Air Power at the Turn of the Millennium

The Canadian Institute of Strategic Studies

Chairman of the Board of Directors: Jean Jacques Blais, QC, PC, BA, LLB
President: Alex Morrison, MSC, CD, MA
Executive Director: David Rudd, MA
Associate Executive Director: Jim Hanson, CD, Eng Cert, MA, CET

The Canadian Institute of Strategic Studies provides the forum for, and is the vehicle to stimulate, the research, study, analysis, and discussion of the strategic implications of major national and international issues, events, and trends as they affect Canada and Canadians

The CISS is currently working independently or in conjunction with other organizations in a variety of fields, including international peacekeeping; Canadian security and sovereignty; arms control and disarmament; Canada-US security cooperation; regional security studies; environmental issues; regional and global trade issues.

CISS PUBLICATIONS INCLUDE:

FREE WITH MEMBERSHIP: The Canadian Strategic Forecast
Seminar Proceedings
Strategic Datalinks
Strategic Profile Canada
The CISS Bulletin
Canadian Defence Quarterly
Peacekeeping and International Relations

BY SUBSCRIPTION: The McNaughton Papers

The CISS is an independent, non-profit organization. For membership, seminar, and publications information contact:

The Canadian Institute of Strategic Studies
2300 Yonge Stree, Suite 402, Box 2321
Toronto, Ontario, M4P 1E4
Tel: (416) 322-8128; Fax: (416) 322-8129
E-mail: info@ciss.ca
Http://www.ciss.ca

Air Power at the Turn of the Millennium

Edited by

David Rudd
Jim Hanson
André Beauregard

Canadian Institute of Strategic Studies

The Canadian Institute of Strategic Studies
Copyright 1999

The Canadian Institute of Strategic Studies meets a need for a body of information on Canadian security issues and it promotes public awareness of the significance of national and international developments. The CISS provides a forum for discussion of strategic matters and, through its educational and informational activities, it seeks to improve the basis for informed choice by the public Canadian public.

Canadian Cataloguing in Publication Data

The National Library of Canada has catalogued this publication as follows:

Main entry under title:

Air power at the turn of the millennium.

Proceedings of a conference held in Toronto, Ont., Apr., 1999.
Includes bibliographical references and index.
ISBN 0-919769-89-6

1. Air power - Canada - Congresses. I. Rudd, David, 1969-
II. Hanson, Jim, 1938-. III Beauregard, Andre (Andre Luc), 1970-. IV. Canadian Institute of Strategic Studies.

UG635.C2A53 1999   358.4'00971   C99-932008-4

The CISS wishes to thank the Commandant and staff of the Canadian Forces Staff College for the use of their facilities for the seminar.

Table of Contents

Glossary..vii

Foreword..ix

Opening Remarks
David Rudd..1

The Future of the Canadian Air Force
LGen D.N. Kinsman, CAS..5

Canadian Foreign Policy: The Canadian Forces and Air Power
Dr. Kim Nossal...17

Whither the Royal Air Force?
Wing Commander Philip Greville, RAF..................................23

Air Power and the Revolution in Military Affairs
Dr. Paul Mitchell...31

Forum..49

Canada, NORAD, and Space
BGen William Kalbfleisch...55

The Education of an Air Force: Professional Military Education for the Canadian Air Force in the 21st Century
Dr. Allan English...63

The Canadian Aerospace Industry
LGen (Retd) David O'Blenis..77

Forum..83

Closing Remarks
BGen (Retd) Don Macnamara...91

Documents

The Changing Face of War..95

Air Power Theory..117

Aerospace Doctrine..141

Inter-service Cooperation: Is it the Essence of Joint Doctrine?..........179

Glossary

AIAC	Aerospace Industries Association of Canada
ASTOR	Airborne Stand-off Radar Aircraft
AWACS	Airborne Warning and Control Systems
BMD	Ballistic Missile Defence
BVR	Beyond Visual Range
C2	Command and Control
C4I	Command, Control, Communications, Computers, and Intelligence
CAF	Canadian Air Force
CDIA	Canadian Defence Industries Association
CINCNORAD	Commander-in-Chief, NORAD
CF	Canadian Forces
DND	Department of National Defence
DOD	United States Department of Defense
DPAR	Defence Production Sharing Agreements
ECM	Electronic Countermeasures
ESSM	Evolved Sea Sparrow Missile
GPS	Global Positioning System
HARM	High-Speed Anti-Radiation Missile
ISR	Intelligence, Surveillance, Reconnaissance
ITAR	International Traffic in Arms Regulations
JDAM	Joint Direct Attack Munition
JSF	Joint Strike Fighter
JSTARS	Joint Strategic Airborne Reconnaissance System
MSH	Maritime Shipboard Helicopter
MPA	Maritime Patrol Aircraft
NATO	North Atlantic Treaty Organization
NORAD	North American Aerospace Defence
NMD	National Missile Defence
PGM	Precision Guided Munitions
PME	Professional Military Education
RAAF	Royal Australian Air Force
RAF	Royal Air Force
RCAF	Royal Canadian Air Force
ROE	Rules of Engagement

RMA	Revolution in Military Affairs
RMC	Royal Military College of Canada
RNZAF	Royal New Zealand Air Force
SCONDVA	Standing Committee on National Defence and Veterans Affairs
SDI	Strategic Defense Initiative
SEAD	Suppression of Enemy Air Defences
UAV	Unmanned Aerial Vehicle
UCAV	Unmanned Combat Aerial Vehicle
UNPROFOR	United Nations Protection Force
USAAC	United States Army Air Corps
USAF	United States Air Force
USSPACECOM	United States Space Command

Foreword

The Canadian Institute of Strategic Studies' spring 1999 seminar brought together a group of academics, military officers, students, and interested observers to explore the various dimensions of air power - primarily in a Canadian context. The role of air forces in Canadian and allied foreign and defence policies, the impact of technology, and the challenges of matching limited means to broad ends were among the topics examined. The seminar was unique in that it took place concurrently with a study of the changing nature and role of air power in global affairs by students of the Canadian Forces College in Toronto.

Opening Remarks
David Rudd

General Kinsman, General Gosden, distinguished guests, ladies and gentlemen. It is my pleasure to welcome you to the Canadian Institute of Strategic Studies' annual spring seminar. It is somehow appropriate that we shall be examining air power at the turn of the millennium, as this year marks the seventy-fifth anniversary of the founding of Canada's air force.

As you know, Canada's military air heritage extends beyond the establishment of the Royal Canadian Air Force (RCAF) in 1924. Many Canadian pilots flew and distinguished themselves with Britain's Royal Flying Corps (RFC) during the First World War. Among them was one William Avery Bishop who, aside from being the British Commonwealth's top-scoring ace, was providing air cover for the Canadian Corps' assault on Vimy Ridge 82 years ago today.

Many of you have attended either yesterday's proceedings and/or the mess dinner here at the Canadian Forces College last night. It is certain that the principal topic under discussion has been NATO operations in and around Kosovo, with the heretofore limited success of the Allied air campaign providing much grist for the mill. It is therefore somewhat ironic that a seminar which was planned many months ago should take place at a time when its intended focus is so timely and relevant. But as one who has (unfortunately) ate, slept, and breathed Kosovo for the past two weeks, I want to assure you that my opening remarks are not greatly influenced by events in the skies over that troubled area. Indeed, is worthwhile to remember that we are here to examine various dimensions of air power - not simply the ins and outs of tactical aviation.

Over the past few weeks I have been reflecting on what could be termed the "non-traditional" aspects of air power. Since we will not be discussing these at length today, I though that I would mention a few just

---

Mr. Rudd is Executive Director of the CISS.

as a reminder of the degree to which the lesser-known aspects of air power have an impact on our everyday lives. Many of those present here today travelled by commercial aircraft. These same aircraft fleets could just as easily be transporting our political and corporate leaders to places where they will conduct business which affects us all. Aircraft of various types may be called upon to bring help to the sick and displaced, or to carry the same to places where they can receive help, whether that be at Trenton, Ontario or Sunnybrook Hospital here in Toronto. Another aspect of air power with which Canadians can readily identify is its capacity to aid domestic authorities in overcoming the forces of nature. Images of water-bombers dousing flames threatening a wilderness area, or a helicopter conveying workers to an off-shore oil rig, or plucking seamen off a foundering ship are powerful reminders that the utility of air power extends far beyond the search for contacts or the delivery of ordnance. The common thread running through these tasks is the desire to influence a situation from the air. That indeed is the essence of air power. How we choose to employ aircraft is limited only by our imagination. So rather than viewing air power as the preserve of nation-states, perhaps we should take a step back and contemplate the "power" that the miracle of flight bestows on each of us.

These days, the general public can perhaps be forgiven for conceptualizing air power in military terms. (Indeed, one rarely hears the term being employed by the airlines!) One could argue that this view is encouraged and reinforced by the country's air arm, which, for good reason, views itself as a unique, if not elite, service with a unique responsibilities to the state and a unique corporate character. Our exposure to the air force and to air power is usually limited to the print and electronic media. Occasionally we might have the opportunity to visit an air show where equipment and flying skills are displayed. We must, however, remember that air power - at least the aspects that we will discuss here today - is a serious instrument of policy, employed to achieve a political objective, or, in simplest terms, to influence a situation on the ground, at sea, or at the bargaining table. Since the stakes, in terms of lives and treasure, are high, and since the security challenges we face are multi-dimensional, we must never allow ourselves to be beguiled by technology or jargon, regardless of how impressive they both may be. If we do, we stand to lose our sense of perspective on what air power can and cannot achieve.

Before we commence the day's proceedings, I would like to thank the Commandant of the College, BGen Gosden, and his staff for hosting the seminar. I would also like to recognize LCol Dennis Margueratt and BGen Jim Hanson for their hard work in putting this event together, as well as Andre Beauregard and his team of volunteers for handling the registration and book sales. Ladies and gentlemen, the Canadian Institute of Strategic Studies is grateful that you are here today. We hope that you will enhance our seminar by lending your perspectives on air power to the morning and afternoon fora.

The Future of the Canadian Air Force
LGen David Kinsman

For much of its life, the Canadian Air Force has been extremely focused. Until 1989 this organization in light blue was focused on one threat and one operating scenario. I thank God that we never did anything but rehearse that scenario. Ironically it has been in the last 10 years that we have been more challenged, in terms of diminishing resources on one hand and increasing demand and operational diversity on the other.

Today I am going to discuss two main points: where Canada's air force is today and, where we believe Canada's air force has to go in the future, bearing in mind the factors that will affect us in the future.

Today's Air Force

Before we can discuss where it is that we are going to go, we have to determine where we are today. I will talk a little about assumptions and trends within in the air force, and I will also talk about some of the things that I personally believe are essential for the future. I am not too sure that any of this will be particularly contentious, but as I have said, the goal is to establish a basis for discussion.

First of all, I will define the mission and vision for the Canadian Air Force. The mission is to generate and maintain a combat-capable, multi-purpose air force to meet Canada's policy objectives. The vision has been recently changed from an all-inclusive statement to something that is brief : Proud, Professional, and Combat-Capable. Several members of Course 25 at Canadian Forces College told me that this is a vision with which they can relate as opposed to the previous, somewhat more jargonistic vision. A vision is something that people have to be able to internalize and have going through their head on an ongoing basis. Thus, the shorter the better.

LGen David Kinsman is Chief of the Air Staff.

6 Air Power at the Turn of the Millennium

Now a quick review of the last decade or so. In 1987, the White Paper on Defence was quite optimistic with respect to where we were going, what DND would have by way of resources, and what we would be building for the future. But very quickly thereafter, in 1989, new realities led us in a different direction. You will notice that we have just come out of the fiscal year which hopefully represents the bottom of the ditch. In subsequent years, as a result of funding that was already planned, and some additional funding that came through the federal budget this year, you will notice that we see, if not a sharp increase, at least a line that at the very least maintains our buying power. This is representative only of an inflationary factor to the budget which has been granted to the Department of National Defence by the federal government. This is the first time in years that this has been institutionalized. There may not be as much money as individuals or the organization would like to have, but the good news is that at least we maintain a purchasing and operating power from a standpoint of resources over the years to come.

How does the decrease in the Department of National Defence's

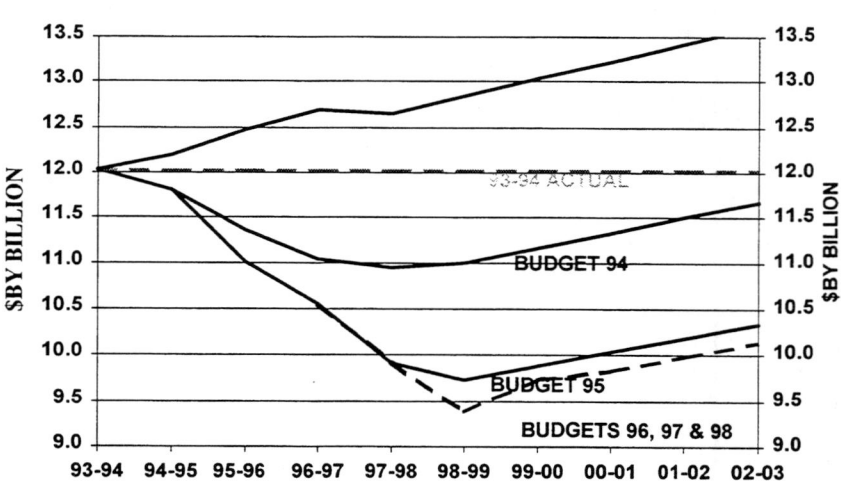

budget affect the air force? Between 1993-94 and 1997-98 the budget of the air force dropped some $275-million a year, or roughly thirty percent in our operating budget. That translates into fewer aircraft, fewer flying hours. In the last 10 years, the number of flying hours alotted to our pilots has significantly decreased.

Notwithstanding this significant decrease in flying time, the challenges have grown from the standpoint of diversity of operations and what it is that we are called upon to do. It is a far more dynamic situation that it was 15 or 20 years ago. By way of amplification, as I said last night at the mess dinner, there is not a combat aircraft in the Canadian Air Force that has not been called upon at least once in the last decade, if not two or three or more times to perform an operational role, and not necessarily the role it was designed for. For example, the Sea King helicopters in Somalia did everything but anti-submarine warfare, and were modified as they were going across the ocean to be able to do things including logistics and night reconnaissance - all of those things that a Sea King was never attended to do. The brand new Griffon helicopters that we bought within the last four to five years have already served in Haiti, Central America after *Hurricane Mitch* this past November and December, and are in Bosnia and Kosovo. The Griffons will be part of any land deployment from now on.

I do not have much to say about the CF-18s. They are now in combat for the second time in nine years. Ironic isn't it? For 30 years we were preparing to go to war and never went. Today many issues are raised at the same time as our budget has been cut back. One of the most common questions is whether we really need fighter aircraft in the longer term. Some say they are too expensive, and ask why do we have them. Lo and behold, in the last nine years we have actually employed them twice.

With respect to the transport fleet, the demand always outstrips supply. There is never enough airlift. The more airlift you buy the more airlift you will be able to use.

Fleet Rationalization

The face of the air force has changed in the last 10 years. In the early 1980s, the air force operated three different type of fighters (Voodoo, Starfighter, and the CF-5 Freedom Fighter) which have now been consolidated into the multi-role CF-18. Helicopter fleets for support to the land forces, which consisted of three helicopters (Kiowa, Iroquois, and Chinook) have now been consolidated into one rotary aircraft. Now if you say that means you are a jack-of-all-trades but master of none, you may do so. But the fact of the matter is that with technology and strapons and so forth, we can do tremendous things with airframes that we might not necessarily have been able to do 15 years ago. The point here is that you can see how we are moving towards that defence policy statement that says that we want a multi-role combat-capable Canadian Forces. The air force is moving in this direction.

In 1989 we had over 20 different fleets of aircraft. Ten years later we have 12 fleets of aircraft. Through our arrangements with NATO flying training, and with our intention to retire other fleets of aircraft, when we get new fleets on line, we will probably have nine fleets of aircraft early in the new millennium. That is a tremendous change, and yet in all of that I maintain that our operational capability will be greater at the end of that process.

With shrinking budgets, the air force has been forced to reduce its personnel. The reductions within the Canadian Forces and the air force have leveled off. Today we have roughly 13,000 people in regular force uniform and somewhere between 2,000-3,000 people in the reserves. Our civilian workforce is down to 3,000. Those are very significant reductions in the number of people doing the job of the air force on a daily basis. In comparison, there were 23,599 regulars, 1504 reservists, and 6,841 civilians in 1989.

Budget Impact - Air Force Personnel Reductions

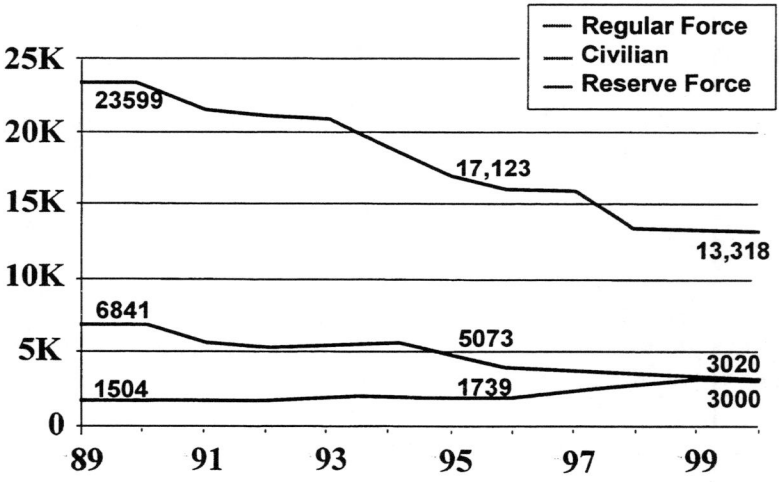

Although we have arrived at the numbers that were prescribed by budgetary reductions, we are not there exactly with respect to the skill sets within those people, and that remains one of my number one priorities. In some classification or trades we have significant excesses of people; in other areas we are tenuously close to the line with respect to sustain ability of skill sets when we go on operations.

The budget of National Defence has also decreased. The air force spends money in three major areas: people, operations and maintenance, and capital. Over the course of the last 10 years, the actual percentage of the budget spent on people and the percentage of the budget spent on operations and maintenance has actually increased, notwithstanding the fact that the real amount of money that we are spending is less as a percentage of the Defence Services Program. Of prime concern is the need to put capital back in balance. Capital is the acquisition of new equipment or major modernization of older equipment. History has proven that if you do not maintain that number at somewhere between 20 to 25 percent of the defence budget, you will eventually end up with equipment that is not able to do the job, which is not safe to operate, which is technologically irrelevant, and which is not capable of functioning. We need to put that back into focus.

From our standpoint there are four major items on the horizon. We are already acquiring the search-and-rescue helicopter. The next priority is the replacement of the Sea King helicopter. We are in the process of finalizing the statement of requirement for this. Our two other major combatants, the Aurora aircraft, a long-range patrol aircraft, and the CF-18, are now in dire need of some technological modernization in order to make them relevant and capable for the next 15 or 20 years. That was part of the program when we bought those airplanes. We selected the CF-18 in 1982 over other aircraft due to its capacity to accommodate itself to new generations of technology. This is part of the overall strategy of maintaining CF-18s in Canada's inventory from about the early 1980s to about the year 2015 to 2020.

Technology is not the problem as long as you have the money and the integration skills. As much as anything else, it is how long the structure of that aircraft that last. How long can you safely fly it?

I always hasten to add that the fortunes of the air force over the last 10 years , notwithstanding budget reductions, have actually been very good. The search-and-rescue helicopters will start to be delivered in about two year's time. In the interim, we have purchased 100 Griffon utility helicopters that are servicing us very well. We have also purchased five Airbus aircraft, four of which have been modified to what we call a combi-mode (in other words, an airplane that is able to take freight as well as people) - a very significant asset from a deployability standpoint. We are in the process of upgrading our Hercules fleet with new avionics, and we have a new pilot training system that is absolutely second to none. It will begin later on this year when the first aircraft start to arrive in Moose Jaw. As you are probably aware, we are slowly but surely attracting an international market to participate in that program with us.

Our traditional commitments have been to NATO and NORAD. Our traditional commitments to NATO included CF-18s, CC-130 Hercules, CP-140 Aurora, NATO EW, CH-146 Griffon, CH-124 Sea King (STANAVFORLANT). NORAD commitments have included CF-18s and Auroras. Today, aircraft are no longer limited to a specific role and mission, as the nature of conflict require flexibility and versatility. But the dynamics of the situations are such that you really do not know from one day to the next where your next commitment is really going to be. It is an exciting time to be working in the air force because whereas before you trained for and concentrated and planned your sustainability around those top-line items, now you can be called upon to take those assets and re-role them or use them in other areas, whether it is for humanitarian reasons or whatever it may be. I have already given some examples.

I have alluded to the fact that there is a significant amount of money required for some of our equipment from a modernization standpoint. So in the search for the right balance between people, maintenance, and equipment, there are some principles that we believe have to be maintained if we are going to make the transition properly. First of all, one of the most significant attributes of air power/aerospace power is its ability to respond quickly. And I do not have to amplify on that given the events of the last couple of weeks in Kosovo. It is absolutely essential in my view that we retain that capability to react and respond quickly. If we allow ourselves to get to a point where it takes us 60 of 90 days to be able to put together a component that may be asked of us by the government and the people of Canada, it is my contention that sooner or later people will be asking why are we buying an air force if you cannot react anymore quickly than any other elements of the CF.

It goes without saying that we have to maintaining a degree of technological advantage. At worst, we have to at least be able to stay in the technological game. Tied in with that is our ability to inter-operate. I will make an assumption that we are not going to deploy combatants overseas on a unilateral basis. It will always be part of a coalition with one or more nations. Key to that is our ability to fit into the command and control structure of that coalition; to be able to communicate while we are conducting operations. Inter-operability is an extremely important principle for us. Also keep in mind that as the resources become tighter and tighter, our job is to render a greater service. The air force does not exist for the air force alone. It exist to assist other services within the Canadian Forces, to other government departments, and internationally.

Fair and equitable treatment of the members of the air force is a personal commitment I made on 1 April of 1998 when I took over the job of Chief of the Air Staff. After some time and increasing discontent, we have addressed a significant chunk of the quality-of-life agenda, as proposed by the Standing Committee on National Defence and Veterans Affairs, the government's response having being tabled at the end of March, 1999. There are some elements that remain to be sorted out, but a very significant part of the recommendations have already been addressed. We must ensure that we maintain a fair socio-economic climate for the men and women of the air force, because without well-trained and well-motivated people, new and sophisticated equipment is really meaningless. There is a balance that we have to achieve there. Great equipment with people who do not feel their talents, their skills, and there efforts are being properly rewarded is not the solution. Conversely, a great compensation package with clapped out equipment is not going to retain people either. There has to be a balance.

Ultimately it comes down to this: quality has to prevail over quantity. So our search is for quality. As I go around the air force and ask men and women which they would prefer to belong too: an organization that is smaller perhaps than what it is right now but that has quality equipment and quality operations; or do you want to belong to an organization that is trying to keep everything that is has had for the last 10 years but cannot do any of it particularly well and we start to slide further and further behind from a technological standpoint, it would be no surprise to anyone here that the answer is always: I want to be part of the quality organization. That involves some tough decisions for us in the future, but that is the direction that we have to go.

Some assumptions for the future. These come from departmental perspectives. We have been doing a lot of work in the Department of National Defence recently on the future strategic outlook and what variables and factors are going to affect us.

War between major powers is extremely unlikely, but conflicts of low-to mid-intensity will persist. The possibility of at least one high-intensity war involving a major power and a regional power is there. Conflicts, either local or regional, will continue. The asymmetric threat, which is the euphemism for technology that is more widely spread and in the hands of small groups - perhaps terrorists or rogue states - is something that we have to know how to contend with.

We have to be prepared to operate in the very low- to high-tech areas. The challenge is not just keeping up mentally with technological change, and how it applies to air forces, but also contending with procurement cycles. How do you keep up when you have a procurement cycle that is 10 or 15 years long, which means that you are going to have three generations of technology in your inventory? How do you rationalize that so that your new acquisitions are technologically current and not two generations out of date the first day that you roll the piece of equipment out.

Speaking of technology, we think that the trends are in areas of increased surveillance, intelligence, reconnaissance capability, long-range precision munitions capability, delivery systems, stealth technology, information, and systems integration technology. Obviously, our doctrine, our force structure, our research and development, our acquisition program, how we operate, all have to react to this.

There are four generic roles of air power. They consist of intelligence collection, rapid movement of goods, the application of coercive force, and control of the medium. I do not see these four generic roles of air power changing. But obviously, battlespace awareness will permit operations by coalition-type forces looking for minimal force and minimal risk. If you listen to the television or the radio in the last two weeks it is fascinating to note that in this country and the United States some 75 percent of people are in favour of sending forces in order to rectify what we see as being an ill, and yet less than 20 percent are prepared to accept any casualties in doing that. This is a situation which is very difficult to come to grips with as a professional military officer.

Another trends is the ability to apply force with the use of all-weather guided precision munitions. This will increase tactical success while minimizing, but not eliminating, physical and political risks. Yet another challenge is the ability to move from one point to the other on the globe rapidly with the quantities of equipment and personnel that you need.

Continuing with the trends, the role of aerospace power will evolve through changes in aerospace organization and control. There are four current trends in the aerospace industry: development of near real-time integrated battlespace awareness; attainment of all-weather precision reach; implementation of enhanced survivability and sustainability, and; expansion and integration of the medium.

The speed with which technological change has impacted upon the structure and resources of Canada's air force, will depend upon the availability of capital investment versus the availability of technology. In other words, there will always be more new technology out there than we can afford. The question is, how does that technology impact upon the environment in which Canada's air force must be prepared to operate? The impact will be immediate even if you cannot necessarily buy all the goodies immediately. Aerospace resources have to be designed for timely employability and precision execution. We absolutely have to invest in the proper technologies, and we need to be deployable and we need to understand that we are almost invariably going to be working with one or more nations in anything that happens off of our shores.

We are going to have a presentation later today on the revolution in military affairs. Let me say just a couple of things about that subject. There are dimensions of the revolution in military affairs that Canada cannot even come close to touching from a financial standpoint; some very specialized areas and equipment flown by our neighbours to the south. This includes surveillance and reconnaissance aircraft that are one-of-a-kind and are so expensive that Canada cannot possibly hope to own them.

What is important though is that Canada positions itself to take advantage of the products of that specialized technology. We must fit them into the command and control structure and be inter-operable so that notwithstanding the fact that those are not necessarily our resources, they become coalition resources which allows us to play a part within the coalition. So interoperability - particularly in command and control and communications - is extremely important.

Another area that I think will be of increasing importance is the whole question of simulation. When we bought the CF-18 in 1982, it had 1970s technology for simulation. It was very limited. The type of technology that is now available not only has a tremendously greater capacity from a fidelity standpoint, it also allows you to interlink. So you can be sitting in your simulator in Cold Lake, Alberta and fly a mission with someone on the other side of the world in realtime. Therefore your capability to train and to train for participation in coalitions, to exercise your doctrines, to exercise command and control is there through means which we not available to us 10 to 15 years ago. We absolutely have to take advantage of that if we want to reduce those operating expenses and so that we can keep up with the technology and interoperability.

Now let me very briefly go through a couple of areas were we in Canada are focussed with our research and development. I have just talked about information management. Electronic warfare, or the protection of our people in an electronic environment is a primary concern. We have some excellent capability in Canada. The difficult is in keeping up once again with the technological jumps. It is something that you owe to everyone you are going to send in harm's way; that they have the very best protection electronically and by other means. The Canadian Airborne Radar Deception System (CARDS) is an area in which Canada leads technologically and we have to take advantage of that.

Surveillance methodologies now allow you do things with aircraft that you would have never been able to do 15 years ago. We can take a Griffon helicopter and take a piece of equipment that was originally designed to take pictures of the Toronto Blue Jays through the top of the SkyDome with gimbal-stabilized cameras, and apply other technologies (not just optics but electro optics and infrared) put that in the Griffon, and you have given yourself a stand-off reconnaissance capability unlike anything we have ever had. Put that in conjunction with the Canadian Army's new piece of equipment, the Coyote, a reconnaissance vehicle, and you have a tremendous ability to look at the battlefield which you never had before. And how do you fold that in with space based and high-altitude UAVs?

With regard to air weapons systems, there are more systems out there than we have money and time to train on. So we have to pick the weapons wisely. Which are the ones that will be of value to us in operations around the world? Which are the ones that are nice to have, but not necessarily in the need-to-have category? And finally, what of Canadian technology? Canada continues to stay ahead in the science of how to counteract g-forces for people in manned aircraft. This is represented by a piece of kit called the Sting anti-g system which allows somebody flying an CF-18, or equivalent aircraft, to be able to sustain up to nine g's without loss of consciousness. Under normal circumstances, a person would loose consciousness after four or five g's. This piece of kit allows us to optimize the man-machine interface.

Surveillance and surveillance from space is something that we can spend a whole day discussing. BGen Kalbfleish will talk to you later about NORAD. From my perspective, our link with NORAD is extremely important in this particular regard. Our access to space-based systems, which gives us knowledge of what is happening is space, is very much enhanced by our relationship in NORAD.

The Essentials for the Future

The air force must be able to generate, employ and sustain high-quality, combat-capable, inter-operable, and rapidly deployable task-tailored forces. We must exploit leading-edge doctrine and technologies to accomplish our domestic and international roles in the battlespace of the 21st century. The following is a list of other essential components.

- **Decisive Leadership:** develop a leadership climate that reflects the value and diversity of members, one that trains and prepares our leaders to lead decisively, manage effectively, and optimize the use of resources in a demanding and changing future. We must also ensure that our personnel have the right learning and education to operate anywhere in the high-technology battlespace of the 21st century.

- **Modernize:** acquire and operate modern combat capabilities that embrace the Revolution in Military Affairs and absorb leading-edge doctrine and technologies that exploit Canada's technological and competitive advantages.

- **Globally Deployable/Responsive:** ensure the combat readiness, global deployability, and sustainability of the air force.

- **Inter-operable:** Maintain and strengthen our relationships and inter-operability with the air forces of our principal allies, particularly the United States Air Force, including doctrine, training, C4I, materiel and logistics.

- **Effective Stewardship:** Adopt an approach to planning and management, focused on operational requirements, encompassing intellectual, knowledge, financial, materiel and infrastructure resources, which enable us to deliver the most cost-effective program and to respond rapidly and effectively to unforecast changes.

- **Valued Partnerships:** Foster greater consensus on defence and security challenges with a view to developing a strong collaborative approach with other government departments and private industry

Air Power and Canadian Foreign Policy in the Post-Cold War Era
Dr. Kim Richard Nossal

My task this morning is quite limited, and it is limited in the first instance by expertise or, more properly, the lack thereof. For whatever expertise I might claim lies not in the area of military affairs, but rather in the area of foreign policy.

Thus my purpose is to present some thoughts on the role of air power in contemporary Canadian foreign policy. In particular, as we begin to discuss the future of air power in Canada at this seminar, I want to ask a simple question: Do we have the right kind of air power for the kind of foreign policy we are pursuing in the post-Cold War era?

Let me preface my remarks with an observation, one that is perhaps exceedingly obvious, but one which nonetheless should be made explicit. And that is that I take it for granted that air power must have rational and instrumental purposes. A country does not simply maintain an air force for its own sake, or because it is the thing to do, or because it is expected by others. On the contrary, the purpose of air power is to support foreign policy broadly conceived, ie., for the defence of the country, for the defence of the country's allies, and to support other foreign policy objectives.

Thinking about an air force in these terms is important, for it begs the question: what kind of air force does one need given the policy objectives embraced?

In the Cold War era, Canadians found this questions relatively easy to answer. We needed interceptors for the defence of North America, and ground attack/air superiority jet fighters for possible use in Europe. An airlift capability was needed for the commitment to the defence of Norway through the Canadian Air/Sea Transportable (CAST) Brigade Group. We also needed rotary-wing aircraft for anti-submarine

---

Dr. Kim Nossal is a professor of political science, McMaster University, Hamilton, Ontario.

warfare (ASW) purposes. And, as Canada's *metier* in peacekeeping developed, there was a need to create an airlift capability with a peacekeeping twist. Likewise, as governments became more concerned with Arctic sovereignty and fisheries management, a maritime patrol capability was needed, one that could mesh with search-and-rescue capability. Helicopters were needed for search-and-rescue, anti-submarine warfare in the North Atlantic, and for tactical support, particularly in peacekeeping missions.

The air force structure that evolved during the decades of the Cold War more or less reflected those policy needs:

- For its North American and European roles Canada acquired and maintained squadrons of Voodoos and Starfighters, eventually replacing both of them with a single multipurpose fighter, the CF-18;
- A fleet of CF-5s was acquired, eventually primarily for training purposes;
- the ASW, surveillance, and sovereignty protection role were conducted by Argus, and then Orion long-range patrol aircraft;
- Sea Kings, Labradors, Kiowas, Twin Hueys, and Chinooks were acquired for a range of activities requiring rotary-wing aircraft;
- CC-130 Hercules and Boeing 707s and then Airbuses were acquired for airlift;
- Air-to-air refuelling capability was also developed.

To be sure, one could always argue (and many did) that there were never enough aircraft to do the many jobs assigned to the air force properly. In other words there was, from the mid-1960s on, an increasing commitment-capability gap. And one could always argue that a succession of governments, Liberal and Conservative, did not pay enough attention to appropriate replacement programs for each of these weapons systems. But by and large it can be argued that the air force we had during the Cold War fitted the foreign and defence policy objectives of Canadian governments during that period.

However, this relatively comfortable fit came to an end with the end of the Cold War. No longer was it so clear what Canada was to develop air power for. No longer was it clear what kind of air power, if any, Canada needed.

After 1991, much of the strategic threat that had underwritten the shape of the air force disappeared. The European theatre was transformed. Faced with the end of the Cold War, the Mulroney government withdrew Canadian forces from Europe, motivated primarily by the prospect of saving money. Moreover, the prospect that Canada would have to commit force to the European theatre became such a remote possibility that the government never augmented airlift capacity to compensate.

The decline of the Soviet threat, and then the transformation of the USSR in 1991 also altered the strategic equation in North America. While an interception capacity was still needed, its importance was clearly downgraded.

Given the shift in the strategic balance, the new Liberal government that took office in 1993 had a very different conception of the importance of air power for Canadian foreign policy. In this, the Chrétien government took a number of cues from the Canada 21 Council, a group of academics and other experts headed by Janice Stein, who is now the chair of Lloyd Axworthy's advisory council. In their report, the Canada 21 Council left in no doubt about their view of the importance of air power in the post-Cold War Period.[1]

Consider their recommendation 23: "That Canada choose to abstain from any international operations that include the possibility of attacks by heavy armoured formations, heavy artillery, or modern air power."[2]

Or other recommendations:

- That the air force be reduced from 72 to 24 operational aircraft;
- That the squadron of 20 aircraft for operational training be eliminated;
- That the number of fighter training aircraft be reduced from 30 to 20;
- that the strategic transport (Airbus 310s) be eliminated;
- And that the only things that be maintained be maritime helicopter, three maritime patrol (surveillance) squadrons; four Search and Rescue and three tactical support (CC-130s) squadrons.[3]

It is true that the 1994 Defence White Paper did not go as far as the Canada 21 Council would have liked. Indeed, it explicitly rejected the idea of a "Constabulary force" - "one not designed to make a genuine contribution in combat"; instead, it embraced multi-purpose, combat-capable forces- fighting alongside the best, against the best."[4] However, the government nonetheless took a decidedly jaundiced view of air power. This can best be seen by the decision enunciated most clearly in the 1994 White Paper on defence - to cut those parts of the air force designed to project air power. Fighter forces were to be cut by 25 per cent; the CF-5 fleet was to be retired; the flying rate was to be reduced; and the number of operational fighters was reduced form 72 to between 48 and

60.[5]

Five years on, we can ask: do we have an air force appropriate for the kind of foreign policy objectives embraced by the government? The government's 1994 White Paper was not short of foreign policy objectives to be pursued using the armed forces. Of particular importance was the goal of contributing to international security, a broad objective that included participation in multilateral operations, responding to threats to international peace and security, peacekeeping missions, and what the government unambiguously called "enforcing the will of the international community."

But if we look at what kind of force structure the government has embraced to meet those objectives, two points stand out:

First, all of the multilateral operations enforcing the will of the international community involving Canada have heavily depended on air power. From the Gulf War of 1991 to the efforts of American forces to bring the clan of General Aideed to heel in 1993, to the efforts to unseat General Cedras in Haiti, to the use of NATO's air power to pressure the Bosnian Serbs in 1995, to the threat and use of force against Iraq throughout the 1990s, to the use of bombing and close-air support against the forces of the Federal Republic of Yugoslavia in 1999, there is an unbroken thread in all of these missions: the importance of air power to achieve foreign policy objectives.

Likewise, if one looks at peacekeeping or peacemaking operations, we see another unbroken thread: the importance of strategic airlift and transport capability to move troops, supplies, fuel, and refugees. Whether it is flying into Somalia or supplies into Sarajevo, or flying armoured personnel carriers to Uganda for use in Rwanda, or trying to mount a humanitarian rescue mission in the Great Lakes region of Africa, or refuelling fighters in the Persian Gulf, or flying refugees out of the Kosovo borderlands, we can see the necessity of this kind of air power.

In other words, air power continues to play a crucial role in implementing foreign policy objectives, even though the strategic equation has changed so dramatically since the Cold War.

The second point is that the Canadian government is using an air force structure designed for Cold War operations, not the post-Cold War environment.

The government's White Paper in 1994 embraced the idea that Canada's air power contribution to multinational operations anywhere in the world would be a wing of fighters and a squadron of tactical support aircraft.[6] Is this all we need in an era when the projection of power by those alongside whom we find ourselves involves not merely the kind of precision bombing CF-18s are now capable of and maintaining air superiority in no-fly zones? Or do we need to rethink what an air force designed for a post-Cold War should look like? In other words, do we need fighters like the CF-18 for air superiority, interception in North America, and precision bombing of the sort we are presently engaged in? The answer, I think, is self evidently yes. But does an air force operating in a post-Cold war environment also need a range of other equipment for diverse missions of the kind that we have seen in the 1990s. Again, consider the Gulf War and its nine year aftermath, the Somalia mission, UNPROFOR in Bosnia, the Haiti mission, the Rwanda mission and its immediate aftermath, or the Kosovo mission. And consider whether limiting Canadian air power to the deployment of a fighter designed for Cold War tasks is appropriate.

Is it time to think about revising the 1986 Senate report on national defence, and dramatically expanding Canada's airlift capability? Is it time to think about the appropriateness of trying to make do with a single multipurpose fighter whose purposes are in fact quite limited? Is it time to think about acquiring a rotary-wing aircraft that is combat capable-precisely for those missions involving enforcing the will of the international community?

Such questions are all the more pointed if we accept that the first decade of the new millennium is going to look much like the last decade of the old one. We are in a new strategic environment. I do not much like the expression "post-Cold War" but I cannot think of an appropriate alternative that captures the essence of a unipolar system dominated by a power like the United States.

And it can be argued that for Canadians it is imperative to keep the US engaged internationally, to work to prevent Americans from closing up shop and retreating to a fortress North America. And there can be little doubt if there is one factor that is most likely to prompt the Americans to withdraw from the international system, it is the belief that others in the international system - particularly their allies - are unwilling to share the burden of managing the post-Cold War environment. And it seems to me that for Canadians, it is very much in our interests to abandon a 30-year tradition of trying to get by by devoting as little as we can get away with to the maintenance of international order, and instead to begin to step forward and offer to help share the burdens of that post-Cold War environment.

And it seems to me that one of the ways that Canada could share those burdens is by acquiring air power appropriate to the kind of strategic environment we face today rather than the kind of strategic environment we faced after the Second World War.

Notes

1. Canada 21 Council, *Canada and Common Security in the Twenty-First Century* (Toronto: Centre for International Studies, University of Toronto, 1994)
2. Ibid., p.64.
3. Ibid., p. 81.
4. *1994 Defence White Paper* (Ottawa: Minister of Supply and Services Canada, 1994) p. 13
5. Ibid., p. 48.
6. Ibid., p. 39.

Whither the Royal Air Force?
Wing Commander Philip Greville

When I saw the title of the presentation, "Whither the RAF", it initially gave the impression that either there is a problem with the long-term future of the Royal Air Force, or is the long-term future of the Royal Air Force even being examined. Ladies and gentlemen, I can tell you that nothing could be further from the truth. What I intend to discuss is the British air power systems that we will be employing into the next century. I will also touch on the recent British Strategic Defence Review, and I am also going to mention some of the enhancements we have underway to improve our joint capabilities. I will describe some of the new air power systems that we intend to bring into service, and I am also going to touch briefly on the new joint battlefield helicopter command, and finish off with a few words on what we propose with *Joint Force 2000*. Those two last points were direct results of our Strategic Defence Review.

I find it quite interesting, given General Kinsman's presentation this morning, that our two air forces have been doing the same thing, and have come up with the same four factors. When we looked during the Strategic Defence Review about what our air power priorities should be into the 21st Century, the four we came up with are remarkably similar to those of the Canadian air force. We are just using different phraseology.

These are the four that I am to run through: information exploitation (referred to as information dominance by the Americans); mobility; air superiority; and; all-weather attack.

Information Exploitation

The first project that I want to talk about is this new aircraft that we intend to procure in the very near future. The Airborne Standoff Radar Aircraft (ASTOR) is the name of the program. This will be the UK's

---

Wing Commander Philip Greville is the Deputy Director of Studies (RAF) at Bracknell, UK.

version of the American Joint Strategic Airborne Reconnaissance (JSTAR) system. We are talking about battlefield/theatre surveillance and target acquisition to pick up hostile moving targets on the ground - including tanks and armoured personnel carriers - with an all-day; all-weather capability. It was a joint air-land requirement because the British Army sees this as a crucial factor for success on the future battlefield.

We are currently examining three possible solutions to fulfil this requirement and there are three aerospace conglomerates bidding to fill it. We plan to buy four or five aircraft. They are all based on a small executive jet. The Ministry of Defence will be making the decision on who will win the contract in the very near future.

Another system is called the RAPTOR, a tactical reconnaissance pod. It is an electro-optical long-range oblique photography system. We are going to put this pod on our new GR4A Tornadoes. The original order is for eight pods, with a larger order in the near future. The in-service date (ISD) is December 2001. We hope to build this capability for the Eurofighter aircraft.

Moving on to an aircraft that we do have in service at the moment, and which is serving us exceptionally well, is our E-3D Sentry aircraft based in Waddington. This is our way of obtaining an air picture. It is currently flying missions over Kosovo. What we are looking to do is to improve this system for the future. Thus we have initiated a radar improvement program, just to make sure that we are keeping abreast with the developments in surveillance technology. We are also going to put an updated air defence suite on this aircraft, and generally improve all the capabilities and mission systems in the back of this aircraft too. What we want to move to now is an airborne command and control system, similar to that used by the United States. Specifically, the RAF wants to develop the E-3D and try to get another console and one or two work stations in the back of the plane to give us a true airborne-to-sea capability. Linked into that is a joint battlefield digitization program and the joint tactical information distribution system, which is a datalink that sends information from the E-3D aircraft into the cockpit of our combat aircraft, down to our ground stations, and to some of our Royal Navy ships at sea.

Air Mobility

I will spend a little more time on the topic of air mobility because we had to look very closely at our air transport capabilities, both strategically and tactically in the Strategic Defence Review. Because we are moving to a more expeditionary style of warfare, we realized that our current fleet of Hercules aircraft in the tactical role were actually getting well past their 'best before' date and are really due for replacement. Many of you are aware that we have gone ahead and purchased the C-130J, the latest version of the Hercules. The RAF is really quite pleased with this new version of the Hercules. We are planning to start taking delivery of these aircraft in the year 2000. The first group will cost in the region of 2.2-billion pounds.

We also have to look into the future of air transport. We have a program called the Future Transport Aircraft, and one of the things that we are considering is going ahead and buying more of the C-130J Hercules. However, there are other transport aircraft that can also fulfil our requirements. Many of these options are under review. We want to move towards getting that second tranche of transport aircraft into service in the year 2005.

Air mobility is a very important element of the Strategic Defence Review, because the United Kingdom is developing our joint rapid-reaction forces. We realize that the air force did not have the strategic airlift required to get the joint rapid-reaction force away from the UK homeland or from our bases in Germany to where they might be required in the future. In order to overcome this severe operational limitation, we have decided that we are going to lease four C-17 jet transports from the US. We intended to do this from the year 2001, and this project is now quite well advanced. I am really looking forward to getting this aircraft into service, and it will be our major strategic airlift capability for the foreseeable future. But what we have to determine is how we can fulfil this capability over the long-term. Because we are only intending to lease these C-17 aircraft or its equivalent, we will begin to hand back those aircraft as the new future transport aircraft is purchased and comes into service.

In terms of mobility, you will be well aware that the RAF has a major air-to-air refuelling capability. We do regard ourselves as an air-to-air refuelling force, and most of our combat aircraft are capable of air-to-air refuelling. The aircraft that we are using as air refuellers are very old VC-10 aircraft and the younger Tristar aircraft. Both are getting very expensive to maintain, and their serviceability rates are beginning to drop off. This sends alarm bells ringing; it must be time to look seriously at replacing theses aircraft. This project is called The Future Strategic Tanker Aircraft, and it will be our primary air-to-air refuelling aircraft of the future. We are looking to replace the VC-10 and the TriStar in 2009 or sooner.

We have to find the cheapest option to fulfil this requirement. We are assessing if it will be possible for a civilian company to actually own and operate these aircraft, and see if we can lease the air-to-air refuelling services from that third party when we actually require it. Personally, I can see a number of severe limitations in following this particular route, and I think that most people in the air force (and certainly those in our air-to-air refuelling fleets) would much prefer for the RAF to purchase their own aircraft, operate them, maintain them, and fly them with RAF aircrew. However, this is the most expensive option, and might not be viable for the future. Thus, we have to keep an open mind and explore carefully all these options so that we can obtain the best value for our money.

Also on the mobility side, we are very pleased that the RAF is also getting the Merlin helicopter. It will be going into service with the Royal Navy as well. The RAF will be receiving 22 of these aircraft, and will begin to take delivery of the Merlin in the year 2000, moving to a full operational capability in 2002. Merlin will be used in the support helicopter role.

We also fly the Chinook helicopter. At the end of this year we will be taking delivery of six new airframes, which is a updated version of the Chinook that we are currently flying. More importantly, we are buying eight of the new Mk 3 Chinook helicopter which is specially equipped to support our special forces. The helicopter will have an air-to-air refuelling capability. This will be the first time that the RAF has had a helicopter capable of air-to-air refuelling. Hopefully in the future we might be able to look forward to developing our own combat search-and-rescue capability.

The Joint Helicopter Command is a direct result of the Strategic Defence Review and will result in a tri-service organization. We have decided that the commander of this force will be an RAF Air Vice-Marshall. We intend to put all the battlefield helicopters, the small number of Royal Navy helicopters in support of our Royal Marines, and all the RAF support helicopters into this one joint force, along with the new Apache attack helicopters that the British Army will be getting in the near future. So the new command will be under an RAF officer, but under the budgetary responsibilities of the British Army and their Headquarters Land Command. Thus you can see that we are truly going into a joint environment with our support helicopters. Some will say that this has been long overdue.

Air Superiority

Our next air power priority involves air superiority. At the moment the aircraft that we are using is the Tornado F3, the fighter version of the Tornado. It has been in service for quite a while now. We have decided that we have to keep this aircraft operational and updated for quite a few years to come, while we gradually phase the aircraft out and bring in the new Eurofighter combat aircraft. The current fleet of Tornado F3s will undergo several significant modifications. We will put new missiles on the aircraft, including the Advanced Medium Range Air to Air Missile (AMRAAM) and the Advanced Short Range Air-to-Air Missile (ASRAAM). I will describe this further later on. We are also updating and improving the air-to-air radar system, and we have also introduced the Joint Tactical Information Distribution System, which was mentioned earlier. It enables the aircraft to receive important information for other aircraft, including the RAF E-3D. We are also going to update the Identification Friend or Foe (IFF) system.

The star of the show will be the Eurofighter. This is going to be the most important aircraft addition to the RAF in the foreseeable future. The Eurofighter is a multirole combat aircraft, which should be operational by 2004. We will take delivery of some aircraft before that date. In total, we will receive 234 airframes arriving in three major batches. On the weapons side, the major weapons for this aircraft, certainly in the air-to-air role, will be the Beyond Visual Range Air-to-Air Missile (BVRAAM) and the Advanced Short Range Air-to-Air Missile (ASRAAM). In time, this aircraft will be developed further to have a reconnaissance capability and a ground attack capability in order to be a true multirole combat aircraft.

Just a few words about some of these missiles that we have coming into service in the near future. The Advance Short Range Air-to-Air Missile is going to be purchased from Matra and British Aerospace in the UK. As I have said already, these missiles will go on the Tornado F3 and the Harrier. It will also be one of the major weapons of the Eurofighter. I was quite intrigued when I read some of the statistics that have come out of the trials of this particular missile. The manufacturers said that it would be an exceptionally fast accelerating missile. Having pressed the trigger in the cockpit to actually launch the missile, the ASRAAM could be 10 kilometres away from the aircraft in 12.5 seconds. This is a staggering capability. On the Eurofighter, because the pilot will be wearing a helmet-mounted sight, he will be able to fire the missile over his shoulder and attack enemy aircraft in a quite large envelope all around his aircraft.

All-Weather Attack Aircraft

The final important RAF air power priority is the precision and all-weather attack capability. The current workhorse for this is the Tornado GR4, and we are very much a Tornado air force at the moment. We began the process of updating this aircraft last year. We are taking our current Tornado GR-1 version - our bomber and ground attack aircraft - for a complete update at British Aerospace. This update includes new engines and new systems. On the avionics side they will receive a new forward looking infra-red system and a better, more usable heads-up display (HUD) for crews. They will be night capable with night vision goggles and a good updated Global Positioning System (GPS). On the weapons side, we will be launching the Paveway III laser guided bomb from this aircraft and we will also introduce two new weapons systems, the Storm Shadow and Brimstone, which are mentioned below.

The Harrier GR-7 is currently seeing duty over Kosovo. We are looking in the future to keep updating the Harrier to ensure that it has the operational capabilities that we require. We are considering updating the weapons aiming computer. We will be introducing the Brimstone, which is an anti-armour missile, and this aircraft also has the capability of launching laser-guided bombs. We also believe that the engine and canon should be updated.

It is equally important to spend the money to keep updating the defensive Electronic Warfare (EW) systems of all our combat aircraft.

I will just take a minute to introduce the Westland Apache Attack Helicopter that we are buying for the British Army. As far as air power is concerned, we are really not just talking about the Royal Air Force or the Royal Air Force systems, but of course, the Army and the Royal Navy. The Apache helicopter is a very exciting development for the Army, and they cannot wait to get their hands on this particular piece of equipment. Delivery to the British Army should begin at the end of 2000. Altogether, the Army will receive 67 Apache attack helicopters. The Apache will replace the elderly Lynx helicopter with its TOW missile in the anti-armour role with the Hellfire missile. This system might become the close air support asset for the British Army in the future. However, this has not yet been decided as it is still under review.

A crucial development for the Royal Air Force is a missile that we have named Storm Shadow. For the first time, the RAF will be able to field a long-range stand-off missile that we will be able to launch from some of our combat aircraft. The missile will be in service in 2002. It has a range in excess of 200 nautical miles, and you can describe it as a miniature version of a cruise missile for the RAF. It is important that we obtain this stand-off capability because it means that we can keep our launching aircraft some distance away from the target area, perhaps in less hostile area, and launch a missile to go and do all the dirty work. It is being made by Matra British Aerospace in the UK. It is based on the Matra Apache system. It is not just for the Tornado as we are going to develop and field this system for the Harrier and for the Eurofighter in the future as well.

Here are just a few facts about the important Brimstone weapon system. It will be our future anti-armour system for the year 2001. The missile will be able to be utilized by both the Harrier, Tornado, and future Eurofighter fleets.

The Maritime Side

We have began a program to modify our current fleet of maritime patrol aircraft, the Nimrod. This program is called the Replacement Maritime Patrol Aircraft. We have decided that we will take the aircraft, send it back to British Aerospace and completely update it with new systems, new wings, new cockpit, and then bring the aircraft back into service on a rolling replacement basis. This is well underway. We are looking for an in-service date of 2005 for our completed, updated version of the Nimrods.

I would like to just touch on the future carrier-borne aircraft and its importance for both the Royal Air Force and the Royal Navy of the future. One of the important things that came out of the Strategic Defence Review was a general declaration that we will go ahead and replace our three fairly small aircraft carriers currently in service with the Royal Navy with two medium size aircraft carriers (approximately 40,000 to 50,000 tonnes). The Royal Navy is really on board for this project, and cannot wait for us to go down this particular route. What we intend to do is replace the Navy version of the Harrier and the RAF Harrier with the same aircraft that will be capable of operating off the new aircraft carriers and from land bases. This project is in the early stages, as we have not decided which aircraft will fulfil this requirement, and it will be some time before we are actually in a position to make such a decision. Going hand-in-hand with this project is the design of theses new aircraft carriers. Thus there is a great deal of expenditure here and obviously we need to make the right decisions and in good time.

In terms of possible aircraft for the carrier fleet, we are currently looking very closely at the Joint Strike Fighter to fulfil this role. British Aerospace is also examining the possibility of developing the Eurofighter combat aircraft into a naval/maritime version to operate from aircraft carriers.

Let me just finish off with a few words on Joint Force 2000, which was forecast in our Strategic Defence Review. Our intention is to merge the Harrier forces of both the Royal Navy and Royal Air Force into one joint force. This really should not be too difficult as we have been operating RAF Harriers off our aircraft carriers for quite a number of years. If you look back in history, you will remember that we were flying Harrier aircraft off our carriers in 1982 during the Falklands War. It is a shame that we did not examine the feasibility of taking this a step further. It is our intention to formulate Joint Force 2000, hopefully for 1 April 2000, and merge these forces into one. It will initially be commanded by a Royal Navy Flag. The whole force will come under RAF Headquarters Strike Command. This new force and will be capable of air defence using the Royal Navy Sea Harrier and the RAF's GR7 Harrier and will have a land attack capability as well. Therefore, we will have a significant capability by merging the two forces. Their home bases will be RAF Corresmore when they are not deployed away on the carriers.

Let me finish off with something that we are looking at for the very long-term. This is based on our requirement to replace the Tornado aircraft, sometime around the year 2018. Many of you are aware that if we do not begin the process right now, we will never actually get the aircraft that we will require in that time frame. This project is called the Future Offensive Air System (FOAS), and we are looking at all the possible ways of fulfilling a deep precision strike capability for the RAF of the future. It must also have a reconnaissance capability. We are looking at three particular options. The least exciting of the options is acquiring stealth aircraft manned possibly with just one crew member and carrying weapons in internal bomb bays. We are also considering the possibility of operating a large aircraft, like a C-17 or a jumbo jet converted into a military aircraft, with a massive cargo bay that you could fill up with air-launched cruise missiles. We would be operating similarly to the present-day United States Air Force with their fleet of B-52 bomber-launched cruise missiles. More importantly, we are also looking for the first time at an unmanned combat air vehicle to fulfil this requirement. It is the first time the Royal Air Force is seriously considering using an unmanned vehicle in a combat role.

We have a long way to go before we get to that stage, but the preliminary studies have begun on all three of those options. Because we are looking to replace the Tornado, and the project will be really quite expensive, we have to approach it in collaboration with European partners, perhaps the NATO members currently flying Tornadoes.

The Revolution in Military Affairs and the Canadian Air Force
Dr. Paul T. Mitchell[1]

"We had to make war as we must; not as we would like to"[2]
Field Marshall Lord Kitchener

The hottest thing in military literature these days is not a new weapons system or strategy. It is vaguely defined hodgepodge of technologies, doctrines and organisational concepts know as the Revolution in Military Affairs (RMA).[3] For Canada, blessed with a secure strategic environment and a meager defence budget, the RMA often seems like science fiction. Indeed, from some perspectives, the RMA must seem more like a curse than an opportunity for the Canadian Air Force (CAF).

In 1916, commenting on the conduct of operations on the Western Front, Kitchener made his now famous comment on the dictates of military necessity as opposed to the requirements of military theory. For the air force, the RMA threatens to turn his statement on its head. Professional military requirements would seem to call for a level of operational capability that may no longer be sustainable given the constraints placed on the Canadian Forces by the annual budgetary figures. Kitchener's dilemma for the air force is that advances in technology may place the capability to conduct even modest air operations at risk: how can a small air force conduct air operations in an age of "systems of systems"?

As a case in point, the air force of the future is currently being placed at risk by the air force of the present. Announcements made in November 1998 noted that CF-18s will be getting a $1.2-billion upgrade, however, budgetary limitations will force that modernisation to be carried out over the period of at least a decade, and may require the sale of 22 of the CF-18s currently in inventory.[4] While the CF-18 is currently capable of flying coalition missions, the Hornets may find themselves

---

Dr. Paul Mitchell is the Deputy Director Academics at the Canadian Forces College, Toronto, Ontario.

constantly on the verge of rust-out with the long lead times for the modernisation that have had to be adopted, and thus potentially excluded from future operations, much as they were in the 1995 operations over Bosnia.[5]

Even as the air force struggles to simply modernise its existing force, the RMA is forcing hard choices onto the air force of the future. If funds are hard to find to simply keep existing aircraft flying, how much harder will it be to fund the procurement of future classes of fighter aircraft (to say nothing of patrol aircraft, helicopters, and transport aircraft)? Of course there is the possibility that the RMA may offer solutions to the dilemma faced by the CAF. New technology may lower personnel costs and there is always the hope that operations and maintenance (O&M) costs may be lowered as well. For technology such as unmanned aerial vehicles/unmanned combat air vehicles (UAV/UCAVs), this may indeed be possible. However, for the vast majority of the concepts and technology dealt with under the rubric of RMA, the costs associated with them are simply so great as to preclude nations like Canada from participating.

An additional concern for Canada is the need to get it right. Writing of an air force facing similar resource and strategic dilemmas, Sqn Ldr S.A. Mackenzie of the Royal New Zealand Air Force (RNZAF) notes:

> Sound fundamental doctrine is essential for a small air force because of the compromises that must be made. A small air force must make every person, every dollar and every mission count for more. To this end, the understanding and application of doctrine in small air forces must be more rigorous than that for larger forces. Whereas a larger force can sometimes use force structure and size to disguise flaws, a small force does not have this luxury.[6]

Yet at the same time, with all the cold comfort that was provided by the stability of the bi-polar era now missing, it is so much easier to get it wrong in today's uncertain geo-political climate. As Colin Gray notes, the potential for error in our strategic assessment ranges from national embarrassment to significant national damage.[7] Yet the envelope provided by the budget makers is such that the tolerance for error is vanishingly small. All this points to the inescapable fact that the issue of the RMA is far larger than simple technological modernisation. The RMA ultimate forces the questions of what is an air force for, what do we wish to accomplish with military air power in the next century, and how much do we wish to invest? Unfortunately, the RMA literature will provide no guide to answer this question; its concepts are too vague and too centered around American requirements to provide any guidance for force planning in Canada. Kitchener's dilemma requires us to make a fundamental re-assessment of the role of the CAF.

Air War and the RMA

Much of the literature that surrounds the RMA is focussed at a "joint" level.[8] Nevertheless, there is a clear "air" element to the debate that surrounds the RMA. Warden claims that the Gulf War witnessed the birth of a new kind of war. "The coalition conducted the first true 'inside to outside' war beginning with the most important center ring in Baghdad and working its way to the outermost ring."[9] Thus, instead of working from the outside of an enemy's power and destroying forces sequentially, rolling them back in a campaign to strike at the most vulnerable and strategically effective targets located deep within the enemy homeland, air power in the Gulf War hit the most important strategic targets on the first night. The RMA as it relates to air warfare seems to be affecting two distinct areas: the redefinition of mass allowing so called parallel operations, and the elimination of 'sanctuaries'.

The Re-definition of Mass

As in ground operations, the concept of mass is an important one for air campaigns. Forces committed piecemeal to an engagement will have limited effect. Similarly, limited effects on the enemy will allow him to recover quickly, thus eliminating any effect a raid intended to achieve in the first place. An air base hit once a week will have a far different operational capability from one hit twice a day for a week. By massing forces, the air commander can more completely guarantee destruction of a target and thus ensure that any recovery will take longer than time available to have an effect on the ongoing campaign.[10] In the past, mass was achieved both through the weight of ordnance dropped on a target as well as in the number of sorties devoted to a target (concentration of force). Thus, by concentrating air assets over a particular target, an air commander could increase the mass of force delivered to it. In WWII, it was necessary to conduct 1000-plane raids in order to achieve both sufficient concentration and sufficient mass delivered on target. This, together with the need to revisit targets over and over again, meant that the bomber campaign was highly resource-intensive and very sensitive to casualties and competing demands for scarce bomber resources.[11]

Stealth technology and precision weapons redefine the nature of mass, however. The stealth/precision combination allows small numbers of aircraft to operate in areas of incomplete or absent air control, and hit targets using small numbers of weapons. Although not the only aircraft capable of dropping precision guided munitions in the Gulf War,[12] the combination of stealth and precision allowed the F-117s to strike targets that were previously too difficult to reach or hit, particularly on the first night of an air campaign.[13] Targets such as aircraft shelters on defended air bases, air defence operations centres, headquarters, communication nodes, bridges, and revetted armour all became vulnerable to attack, even in the face of an unattrited air defence system.

Forty-two F-117s participated in Desert Storm, flying 1299 combat sorties against targets in Iraq and Kuwait. Of the 1788 strikes against all 12 target categories in the Instant Thunder air campaign plan, 1664 were direct hits for a 92% success rate.[14] In sum, 2% of the air assets available to the coalition flew 1% of the missions, but accounted for 40% of all the targets damaged in the war, without a single casualty.[15]

Each mission itself was a example of economy as well. For example, in a single mission to Basrah, 38 non-stealth aircraft were necessary. Four A-6Es and four Saudi Tornadoes represented the sharp end of the strike, actually dropping ordnance on the target. To get them there, however, they had to be accompanied by four F-4Gs flying a 'Wild Weasel' air-defence suppression mission, five EA-6Bs, 17 F/A-18s armed with high-speed anti-radiation missiles (HARM) missiles, and four additional F/A-18s flying combat air patrols (CAP). The eight strike aircraft hit three aimpoints in the mission. The same night, 20 F-117s attacked 37 different aimpoints in a single mission, supported only by two tanker aircraft, representing a 1200% increase in target coverage using 47% fewer aircraft.[16] In effect, the combination of stealth and precision opened up entirely new mission areas to air planners, allowing nuclear-like decapitation attacks to be made without the recourse to those nasty weapon systems.[17]

The implications of this from a planning standpoint are rather remarkable. First, it allows 'parallel', as opposed to sequential operations to be performed. Thus simultaneous attacks can be made on many high-value targets with little or no need for suppression of enemy air defences (SEAD) to be accomplished beforehand. As such, compression in terms of time and expansion in terms of space can be achieved without sacrificing mass or concentration of force. Simply put, mass and concentration need not imply tonnage and large numbers of aircraft any longer.[18]

Paul Mitchell 35

Breaching the Weather Sanctuary

The combination of Intelligence Surveillance Reconnaissance (ISR), Command, Control, Communications, Computers and Intelligence (C4I), and Precision Guided Munitions (PGM) has the effect of gradually eliminating all remaining 'sanctuaries' that enemy forces can shelter under. Until the introduction of the P-51 in World War II, the Luftwaffe was able to take shelter in distance in that fighter escorts were unable to accompany bombers all the way to the target. Similarly, enemy forces were able to use the night as a sanctuary until the introduction of night vision technology and optronically guided munitions in the Vietnam War. Only the weather sanctuary remains to be breached at the present time. Weather reduced the effectiveness of laser/Infra-Red (IR) guided weapons in the Gulf War. The F-117 only had a 70% hit rate in the first three weeks of Desert Storm, during which the worst weather occurred. Further, half of all sorties had to be either cancelled or diverted during this initial period.[19]

Weather had a detrimental effects on the recent campaign over Yugoslavia.[20] Allied aircraft experienced considerable difficulty in using precision targeting laser designators. Cancelled operations provided lulls in operational tempo which the Serbs seemed to take advantage of. These lulls were used to conceal and disperse their forces, as well as to accelerate the tempo of ethnic cleansing. However, the Kosovo campaign also saw the introduction of new weapon systems that are unaffected by weather considerations. As such, B-2 aircraft have dropped the so-called Joint Direct Attack Munition (JDAM) which is guided using information provided by reconnaissance assets such as the Joint Surveillance Target Acquisition and Reconnaissance System (JSTARS), and coordinates provided by global positioning system (GPS).[21] Thus even the weather sanctuary is gradually being breached, allowing true 24 hour, all-weather operations to be carried out.[22]

While the overall emphasis of the RMA is focussed on enhancing control over the battlefield, the implications of the RMA for air power at the political level are considerable. The promise of the RMA is to increase the speed with which operations can be achieved, thus limiting political risk to nations involved. Similarly, the increased rapidity of operations together with the reduction of personnel possible through RMA developments lessens the exposure and risk to air crews in air operations. From an overall risk perspective, the RMA may enhance the flexibility of decision-makers and military planners by allowing the exploration of a greater range of options for any given situation.[23] Indeed, stand-off precision guided munitions allow a response where none may have been possible previously. The air strikes conducted on Osama bin Laden's training bases in Afghanistan and the alleged chemical weapons factory in the Sudan are cases in point.

Constraints on Small Air Forces: The Future Air Environment

As doctrine manuals are fond of pointing out, the air is a harsh environment. It is becoming particularly so for small air forces. Constrained by budgetary realities, small air forces have seen their operational flexibility cut back progressively in recent years. The high costs of air combat are leading to a renewed interest in the lightweight fighter concept.[24] However, the technical demands of modern air combat are such that this solution is unlikely to pay the dividends that were possible in the late 1970s and early 1980s. Case in point are the challenges posed by beyond visual range (BVR) targeting and weapons speciation.

Force Limiters: BVR

The quest to lower casualty rates and increase the effectiveness of air power is likely to increase the emphasis placed on beyond visual range targeting and engagement.[25] Technologically speaking, BVR engagement is one of the most demanding tasks in air warfare. Long-range air-to-air engagement has been the promise of the missile age since the early 1950s, yet it has never worked as well in practice as it has in theory. The promise of BVR resulted in aircraft like the F-4 Phantom II, designed without an internal gun on the assumption that missiles had rendered the dogfight obsolete. The Gulf War seems to have demonstrated the gradual realisation of this promise, with 40% of all air to air kills being achieved by the AIM-7 Sparrow missile.[26] Friedman points out that BVR targeting worked well against a passive opponent and a "sky full of friendlies" dominated by the all-seeing Airborne Warning and Control System (AWACS) aircraft. However, even here, rules of engagement (ROE) required two separate pieces of electronic identification before AWACS would grant firing authority. The limitations of the F-14's detection systems meant that it was not allowed to use its extremely long-range AIM-54 Phoenix weapon systems.[27]

Technical requirements, especially that of BVR, will penalise those designs which seek economy. Track-while-scan radars necessary for BVR will drive airframe sizes and, to a large extent, costs. Sophisticated avionics will be necessary to enable multiple target engagement and multimode operations, as well as adequate electronic countermeasures (ECM) and enhanced situational awareness. Even in airspace dominated by friendly AWACS aircraft, ROE may require independent confirmation of identity and thus a whole host of Identification Friend or Foe (IFF) related equipment. Indeed, once kit such as heads-up display (HUDs), hands on throttle and stick (HOTAS), radar warning receivers (RWR), ECM,[28] night vision and laser designators are added, the potential lightweight fighter begins to approach the cost and sophistication of most middle-range fighter designs. Such was the recent experience of the ill-fated Northrop design, the F-20 Tigershark, which found a market dominated by the F-16 while offering no extra features and few savings against that design.[29]

Nor is the lightweight fighter challenged by avionics alone. Once BVR is established as an operational requirement, it drives virtually every specification. Thus, long-range missiles are typically far heavier than shorter-range IR-guided missiles, and thus require larger aircraft with greater endurance in order to carry any number of them. BVR will require greater stealthiness in airframes and thus the need for internal carriage of weapon systems (in turn driving larger airframe and engine size). High-performance engines and advanced aerodynamics will still be required should the BVR engagement fail and dogfighting become necessary. As the F-14 example from the Gulf demonstrated, BVR capability is much like a chain, any weak link in the system can undermine the entire system. Thus, capabilities such as BVR impose systemic constraints on aircraft design.[30]

Force Limiters: Operational Design Concepts

The USAF is attempting to deal with the high cost of BVR by re-employing the hi/lo mix concept developed in the mid 1970s. F-22s are meant to establish control of air space and then support lesser aircraft such as older F-16s and the Joint Strike Fighter (JSF). Less capable JSFs will use airborne and space-based ISR/C4I systems to receive their command and control (C2), tactical information and targeting data. This necessarily accepts considerable relaxation in the requirements to operate in a high-threat air combat environment.[31] As currently envisaged, the JSF will not offer revolutionary advances over the present airframes represented by the F-16 and F/A-18. However, the JSF, it is hoped, will offer lower life-cycle costs and the ability to deliver PGMs with greater accuracy.[32]

By virtue of the fact that no other nation seems to be putting money into this particular market niche, the JSF may dominate the force structures of many air forces in the middle of the next century, by virtue of its monopoly in design and cost.[33] However, as a less-than-all-purpose fighter operating in a hostile environment, the small JSF may be restricted in the types of missions it can undertake. In effect, lacking the ability to independently scan air space at long range, a JSF force structure may be incapable of adequately performing sovereignty patrols. Allied JSFs may be entirely dependent on USAF assets simply in order to operate.[34]

Force Limiters: Weapons 'Speciation' and Intelligence

Small air power's flexibility may also be increasingly limited by the so-called 'speciation' of munitions. As Keany and Cohen noted of the Gulf War, as the precision of munitions increases, their tactical flexibility declines. Precision weapons need careful mating against target requirements. Further, speciation creates additional pressure on small air forces unable to maintain large and diverse inventories of precision weapons. Canada's inventory is limited to three types of weapons, the GBU-24 for very hard targets, and the GBU-12 for all others, as well as the Rockeye cluster munition. It is difficult to imagine the Canadian Air Force acquiring the range and mix of munitions available to the USAF or other larger air forces. Such economy obviously has considerable impact on the types of mission that can be pursued by the CAF.

Equally, precise munitions call for highly accurate intelligence to find the targets and their weak points.[35]

Now that bombs can be guided down the air shafts of aircraft bunkers and onto a specific segment of a large bridge, the expertise of structural engineers and a host of other such specialists has become correspondingly important in planning an air campaign.[36]

Parallel operations and munitions speciation, therefore, go hand-in-hand. Parallel operations require precise attacks on key nodes which, when destroyed or suppressed, will have concomitant functional effects on the conduct of the war. In turn, targeting will require critical intelligence to assure that the proper weapon will be applied against each target to maximise the effect of each strike. Indeed, though a strike may be highly precise, it may not guarantee effectiveness if it does not achieve the desired results. Though the RAF was able to hit U-boat pens in Brest throughout the Second World War, only with the development of the 12,000 pound Tallboy bomb were they able to achieve any effectiveness in penetrating the reinforced concrete roofs.[37] Somewhat differently, but with similar lessons for effectiveness, strikes on the Al Tuwaitha nuclear research facility were meant to hinder Iraqi ability to produce nuclear weapons after the conclusion of the war. Only afterwards did it become apparent as to the extent of that research effort and the lack of effect the air campaign had had on it.³⁸ Even when there is visible evidence of a hit on a target, such as a hole in an aircraft shelter, or an explosion on a gun site video tape, this does not in and of itself constitute evidence that the strike has had the intended effect. The shelter may be empty and the explosion may conceal the fact that the munition missed the target.³⁹

Undertaking air-to-ground operations will require an enormous amount of intelligence. Intelligence will not be required solely on orders of battle and force deployments, but will extend down to industrial and social intelligence. Small air forces will be hampered by equally small staffs to undertake this level of detailed analysis. Again, their only solution may be to rely completely on either coalition operations, or on the Americans.⁴⁰

To sum up the air power environment, it is expensive and it is getting more so each and every year. While this discussion has focussed narrowly on fighter requirements, the supporting infrastructure that supports fighter missions such as the training facilities, airlift, air-to-air refuelling, maintenance, and intelligence all make air superiority and air-to-ground operations highly demanding on the nation's pocketbook.⁴¹ Such costs have prompted many to wonder whether the cost of air operations will drive most out of the arena:

> The question is not can air power carry out the mission? The question will be can air power carry out the mission without usurping such enormous resources that the war-making system as a whole remains balanced and effective?⁴²

Since 1911, manned aircraft have had a fundamental impact on the development of warfare. However, the time may be fast approaching when countries will have to make fundamental choices about how to pursue military aims possibly in the absence of manned aircraft. In the early 1970's Norman Augustine, CEO of Martin Marietta predicted:

> In the year 2054, the entire defence budget will purchase just one tactical aircraft. This aircraft will have to be shared by the air force, and navy, three and a half days per week, except for the leap year, when it will be made available to the Marines for the extra day.⁴³

While that state may not have been reached yet by the US armed forces, that particular prospect seems to be staring many small air forces in the face

UAVs: the Poor Man's Air Force?

UAVs have been in existence for some time.[44] Recently, American Predator UAVs have been operating over Kosovo.[45] Nevertheless, the rapid advances in electronics that are driving developments in the RMA have also been having an effect on the development and utility of UAVs. Miniaturisation of electronics, advances in telecommunications, and the potential developments in artificial intelligence have dramatically increased the potential of UAVs. Indeed, the future of combat aircraft may lie in what is referred to as the unmanned combat aerial vehicle (UCAV).

The UCAV concept includes not only the aircraft, but also the ground station and data networks. Human operators are not meant to be simply remote pilots, but mission managers, potentially flying dozens of vehicles. As a result, the craft will need to be autonomous to a considerable degree so as to reduce communication bandwidth requirements. Thus, UCAVs may fly a portion of their mission autonomously, turning control over to managers only during certain portions of their flight profile, or depending on the situation, may be completely self-operating. The UCAV might be either a relatively benign platform carrying stand off weapons, or may be an aggressive, manoeuvrable fighting platform.[46] The UCAV concept, thus, allows for considerable flexibility allowing mission planners to tailor their flight plans to a wide variety of control options.

The principle advantages of the UAV/UCAV concept over manned aircraft are in terms of cost and design. Lacking a pilot, expensive environmental system, cockpits and associated instrumentation can all be eliminated in the UAV/UCAV, generating savings in terms of weight and overall cost. Smaller aircraft entail added benefits in terms of their reduced IR signature and radar cross section.[47] Second, without a human on board, the full potential of aerodynamic design can be exploited, resulting in high speed/highly manoeuvrable aircraft that need make no compromise for the limitations of human physiology. Should a UAV be shot down, resource-intensive and dangerous combat search-and-rescue (SAR) operations need not be launched.[48] Finally, UAV/UCAVs potentially reduce O&M costs by allowing flight managers to train exclusively in simulators, allowing the aircraft to be stored like munitions.[49] Given the cash crunch that many militaries will be facing in terms of capital acquisition in the early part of the next century, the potential for UAV/UCAVs to reduce both personnel and O&M costs is particularly attractive.

Paul Mitchell 41

Challenges to UAV/UCAVs

Nevertheless, UAVs face considerable challenges before they realise their full potential. The most obvious challenge is institutional resistance to the entire concept of replacing pilots with machines. UAVs represent a fundamental threat to one of the most powerful unions within many militaries - the pilot cadre - and more specifically, the fighter pilot community. As such, it is likely that UAVs will be less than enthusiastically welcomed by the military. Without a specific champion within existing military hierarchies, UAVs may have to be foisted onto air forces by civilian managers and legislators even as cruise missiles were in the 1970s. Even then, institutional resistance may see these assets less than effectively employed. One need only look to the debate over the A-10 to see how institutional resistance can affect the operational use of certain assets.

However, significant technological hurdles remain that need to be overcome before UAVs fulfill the promises that have been made for them. Integrating UAVs into the existing military infrastructure may prove equally challenging, irrespective of institutional biases. How situations like air-to-air re-fuelling, recovery of UAVs still loaded with live ordnance, and the provision of alternate recovery fields will be handled remains to be seen.[50] On board ships, a host of problems similarly need to be addressed before the notion of mini-carriers can be taken much further than a purely conceptual stage. In particular, how the control frequencies and equipment of UAV/UCAVs will be affected by the nearby presence of high-powered search and fire control radars needs to be sorted out. How UAVs in 'return home' mode will find their ship as it manoeuvres has yet to be determined. Finally, the simple problem of where to put these aircraft on platforms that already have very limited amounts of space has not yet been addressed.[51]

Most critically, how datalinks with UAV/UCAVs will be managed is a particularly difficult issue. To some degree, bandwidth scarcity will require that UAV/UCAVs be largely autonomous as the volume of data necessary to provide the requisite situational awareness to allow aggressive manoeuvring is likely to be prohibitively high. High altitude endurance (HAE) UAVs offer the potential of real-time reconnaissance for theatre commanders, however these too will eat up huge swaths of available bandwidth. One study suggested that the entire US does not have sufficient bandwidth resources to operate more than one Global Hawk HAE UAV at one time, even when using civilian satellite uplinks. The problem becomes even more critical as other nations adopt UAVs into their force structures and a whole host of civilian and military applications escalate demands on the radio frequency spectrum. In such areas, control of UAVs could be significantly degraded and certainly would open up the potential for enemy attempts to interfere with their missions. The "proliferation of radio frequency communication systems (military and civilian) will make it difficult and expensive for UAVs to meet high expectations for worldwide real time intelligence."[52]

In sum, the UAV/UCAV concept has much to recommend it. However, the potential of these types of aircraft supplanting manned aircraft still remains far into the future. Whether they will arrive in time to offer small air forces a means of avoiding the hard decisions that will be forced on them by extremely tight budget envelopes is unlikely. Whether air forces will have the courage to explore those options should they become available also remains to be seen.

Strategy, the RMA, and the Future of the Canadian Air Force

As we have seen, the RMA raises issues far greater than technical modernisation. Unfortunately, the concepts developed in the RMA literature concentrate on technology and devote little though to the strategic rationales or need for such technology. Colin Gray has criticised this reductionist approach to strategy. He argues that as well as technological superiority, states must demonstrate excellence in fifteen different dimensions of strategy including political leadership, and public support.[53] Thus, ultimately the question of how the RMA will impact the Canadian Air Force cannot be answered by a simple analysis of technology alone. As has been progressively argued here, uncertain roles and utility that surround new technology, as well as the enormous costs associated with both R&D and procurement of it mitigate against a wholesale embrace of the 'revolution'. The simple fact remains that the RMA provides little direction for those charged with making hard decisions regarding the future of the air force in this country.

Certainly, should we wish to continue to participate in international coalition operations as we have over Iraq and Yugoslavia in the past decade, interoperability will require that we adopt portions of the RMA simply to allow our forces to contribute. Nevertheless, our ability to do so will shrink rapidly in the next century as the costs of modernising and maintaining our existing fleet of CF-18s skyrockets, much less the cost of replacing them altogether with something like the JSF. This situation can only worsen to the point that the sharp end of the air force may become entirely dependent on the support of the USAF. US requirements see the JSF operating as a system within a system. Thus, a trade-off can be made given that the American JSF's can call upon assets like

AWACS and JSTARS to assist it in the completion of its missions. Lacking the accompanying kit, Canadian JSF's would be fundamentally hamstrung in their ability to accomplish missions without US support. Without a long-range multi-mode radar, the JSF will be unable to meet Canadian surveillance requirements. Still, with such kit, we may be unable to afford it.

The fundamental problem facing the Canadian Air Force then is that there seems to be no overarching strategic vision to guide the air force through this challenging period. There is nothing that describes what the air force is for or what it is meant to accomplish. The air force's 'vision statement', *Out of the Sun*[54] tells one how the air force seeks to accomplish its missions, but not why, nor more importantly, why this is critical to Canada as a nation. This lack of vision may be simply due to professional myopia: the reasons for possessing an air force are so blindingly obvious that none have considered it necessary to explain it. I would suggest that if this is true, it is incorrect on two accounts. First, to many Canadians, it is not obvious why Canada needs equipment like fighter aircraft. The 'fireproof house' is an overwhelmingly strong metaphorical influence in their global outlook. The need to conduct offensive fighter operations will have to be made very carefully then.

Second, the entire process of thinking about why we need an air force and what it is meant to accomplish will stimulate thought and blow the dust out of conceptual alleys within the air force itself. As the navy found during its re-examination lasting between the appearance of *The Naval Vision* in 1994 and the publication of *Adjusting Course* in 1997, self-assessment can be a very fruitful process.[55] Self-assessment, however, comes with a risk and this leads to the a second possibility as to the absence of a strategic vision for the future of the air force.

In fact it may be may be purely institutional: no one wants to confront the awful possibility that there may, in fact, be no future for an offensively-oriented, independent air arm in Canada. The army could absorb, functionally if not institutionally, the tactical helicopter, the navy the maritime shipboard helicopter (MSH) and maritime patrol aircraft (MPAs), leaving the air force with the decidedly unglamorous role of air transport. While it is possible that fighter operations could eventually be tasked to UCAVs, this would require overcoming significant institutional prejudices against such a concept, to say nothing of the serious technical challenges that still remain in the way of such aircraft. In any case, functional UCAVs are unlikely to make their appearance much before 2015, leaving one to suspect that air combat skills in this country will wither before they come available to save that particular role. The present success over Kosovo aside, fighters are perhaps the most difficult piece of military hardware to justify to the Canadian public.

Dewar notes:

> It is too early to postulate the solution to the new force structure that will permit the Canadian Forces to effectively accomplish the three defence missions in the terms of the RMA.... Before determining the answer, it is necessary to apply intellectual vigour to framing the question about what may be asked of the Canadian Forces and when it may be asked.

Parallel war and precision strikes aside, war will remain a brutal and ugly business in the next century. The question that remains to be asked is, how brutal a business do we wish to take part in? It is this question that needs answering; technological issues cannot be addressed until it is. Military professionals will want to be as capable as possible, however, why have a professional obligation to explain to those not familiar with military operations why this must be so. In a secure country like Canada, Kitchener's dilemma will be an on-going challenge for military professionals. History and geography ensure that it will not fade away any time soon. All the more need for forward thinking and transparent policy on the part of the air force if it wishes to remain in the business of combat operations in the next century.

Notes

1. The opinions expresses are those of the author and do not necessarily represent the views of either the Canadian Forces College or those of the Department of National Defence.
2. Lord Kitchener, address to War Cabinet on the Western Front, 1916. Quoted in Trevor Royle, *A Dictionary of Military Quotations* (London: Simon & Schuster, 1989).
3. For an overview of the RMA, see: A.J. Badcevich, "Preserving the Well Bred Horse", *The National Interest*, Fall 1994; Alvin & Heidi Toffler, War and Anti-War, *Survival at the Dawn of the 21st Century* (New York: Little Brown, 1993); Adm. William A. Owens (USN), "The Emerging System of Systems", *Proceedings,* May 1995.
4. George Koch, "CF-18 Fighters get no new weaponry in $1.2-billion upgrade", *National Post*, December 14, 1998; Sharon Hobson, "Canada Restructures CF-18 Project", *Jane's Defence Upgrades*, Vol. III, No. 3, p. 7; Dean Beeby, "Canada's Aging CF-18 Fleet to get over $1-billion in Improvements", *National Post*, Dec. 14, 1998.
5. Koch, Op Cit; Allan Thompson, "Canada Earns Air War Stripes in Kosovo", *The Toronto Star*, May 29, 1999.
6. Sqn.Ldr. S.A. Mackenzie (RNZAF), *Strategic Air Power Doctrine for Small Air Forces* (Canberra: Air Power Studies Centre RAAF Base Fairbairn, 1994), p. 1.
7. Colin Gray , *Canadians in a Dangerous World* (Toronto: The Atlantic Council of Canada, 1994), p. 10.
8. According to Owens: It is no the kind of conceptual framework that leads into discussions of numbers of Army divisions, or aircraft carriers, or air wings of the supporting infrastructure for those traditional missions of military capability. It is a joint perspective, a framework that frees us from the sterile debates about how many divisions or how many carriers - and permits us to focus on far more important issues such as the character of our forces and the manner in which they can work synergistically toward our military capability. Owens, 1995, Op cit., p. 38.
9. John A. Warden III, "Employing Air Power in the 21st Century", *The Future of Air Power in the Aftermath of the Gulf War*, Richard H. Shultz, Jr., Robert L. Pfaltzgraff Jr. (ed.s) (Maxwell AB: Air University Press, 1992.), p. 78.
10. John A. Warden III, *The Air Campaign. Planning for Combat* (Washington: National Defense University, 1988), p. 34.
11. Ibid., p. 167.
12. The USAF dropped laser-guided bombs (LGB) with their FB-111s and F-15Es. British Tornadoes also dropped LGBs, although RAF Buccanners carried the laser designators. Finally, the USN used A-6Es in precision strikes as well.

13. Thomas A. Keany and Elliot A. Cohen, *Revolution in Warfare? Air Power in the Persian Gulf* (Annapolis: Naval Institute Press, 1995), p. 191-193.
14. *Gulf War Air Power Survey*, Vol. 4, Pt. 1 (Washington: USGPO, 1993), p. 40.
15. Ben Rich and Leo Janos, *Skunk Works* (Boston: Little Brown, 1994), p. 104.
16. Colonel Dave Deptula (SUAF), "Firing for Effect. Change in the Nature of Warfare", Aerospace Education Foundation Defense and Airpower Series paper, http://www.aef.org/fire.html, p. 6.
17. Szfranski notes that concepts of Parallel war seem to be only conventional variants on the Nuclear SIOP. Colonel Richard Szfranski (USAF), "Parallel War and Hyperwar: Is Every Want a weakness?", *Battlefield of the Future: 21st Century Warfare Issues*, Barry R. Schneider and Lawrence E. Grinter (ed.s), (Maxwell: Air University, 1995)
18. Deptula, Op Cit.
19. James A. Winnefeld, Preston Niblack, and Dana J. Johnson, *A League of Airmen: US Air Power in the Gulf War* (Santa Monica: RAND, 1994), p. 124.
20. Michael Evans, "Weather Holds up the Bombs", *The Times*, March 31, 1999. Disappointing results with LGBs eventually forced NATO planners to adopt cluster munitions and low level delivery tactics. John Follain, "Frustrated RAF to use high-risk Cluster Bombs", *The Times*, April 4, 1999.
21. Anne Kornbult, "Inclement Weather Forces NATO to Try New Type of Warhead", *Boston Globe*, March 30, 1999, p. A10.
22. David R. Mets, "Stretching the Rubber Band: Smart Weapons for Air-to-Ground Attack", *Technology and the Air Force: A Retrospective Assessment*, Jacob Neufeld et al (eds.), (Washington: USAF, 197).
23. Colonel John A. Warden III (USAF), "Air Theory for the 21st Century?", *Battlefield of the Future: 21st Century Warfare Issues*, Barry R. Schneider and Lawrence E. Grinter (eds.), (Maxwell: Air University, 1995).
24. Richard Aboulafia, "Are Fighters Meeting Global Market Needs?", *Aviation Week and Space Technology*., p. 1-2. Representative fighters include the F-16A/Bs, Mirage 2000s, Ching Kuos, Av-8Bas, AMXs, Mirage F-1s, Super Entendards, Viggens, A-4s, A-7s, F-5s, Mirage IIIs, and several different types of Russian fighters and Chinese derivatives.
25. Keany &Cohen, Op cit, p. 208.
26. Anthony H. Cordesman and Abraham R. Wagner, *The Lessons of Modern*, *Vol. IV: The Gulf War* (Boulder: Westview, 1996), p. 405.
27. Friedman, Op cit, p. 189. F-14s lacked non-cooperative target recognition capabilities which allow a fighter's radar to determine the identity of an air target based on the blade or compressor turn rate of its engine. F-14s were limited to long range TV and IFF.
28. Sergio Coniglio, "The New Fighter Generation", *Military Technology*, Vol. 16, No. 8, 1992.
29. Air Vice Marshal J.R. Walker, *Air Superiority Operations* (London: Brassey's, 1989), p. 63.

30. Coniglio, Op cit., p. 28.
31. Andrea Nativi, "Combat Aircraft: the New Breed is Coming", *Military Technology*, Vol. 22, No. 9, 1998, p. 4.
32. Aboulafia, Op cit., p. 3.
33. Such dependence may be inevitable in any case as the NATO procedure necessary for modern air operations ensures that allied contributions are firmly under the control of the United States. For an outline of NATO process and rational, see Friedman, Op cit, p. 171-172.
34. Ibid., p. 222.
35. Edward Luttwak, "Air Power in the US Military Strategy", *The Future of Air Power in the Aftermath of the Gulf War* (Maxwell AFB: Air university Press, 1992), p. 24.
36. *Gulf War Air Power Survey*, Vol. 2, Pt. 2 (Washington: USGPO, 1993), p. 45.
37. Ibid., p. 54-56.
38. Friedman, Op cit, p. 253-254; Keany & Cohen, Op cit, p. 219.
39. For a discussion of the sorts of difficulties faced over Kosovo see: John Keegan, "Hard Choices Ahead over 'Soft' Targets", *The Daily Telegraph*, March 29, 1999; Vernon Loeb, "Above Inaccessible Areas, Satellites Track Refugees and Atrocities", *The Washington Post,* April 6, 1999, p. A18; Michael Evans, "Searching High and Low for the Enemy", *The Times, April 6, 1999.*
40. Keany & Cohen, Op cit., p. 220.
41. George & Meredith Friedman. *The Future of War* (New York: Crown Publishers, 1996), p. 252.
42. Ibid., p. 248.
43. UAVs have been used operationally since at least the 1973 Arab Israeli War. They were an important part of the Israeli strike plan against the Syrian IADS in the 1982 Be'kaa Valley campaign where they simulated attacking aircraft, provoking the Syrians to turn on their radar. They also provided critical reconnaissance to Israeli aircraft that allowed them to continue to attacking Syrian missile sites, even after air defence radars had shut off. Finally, UAVs were used extensively over Bosnia during Operation Deny Flight. Lt.Col. David Eshel (IAF Retd), "Suppressing the Threat", *Unmanned Systems*, February 1997; Robert C. Michelson, "The Future is.... NATO. The Road Ahead for UAVs in NATO", *Unmanned Systems*, Winter 1996, p. 11.
44. Michael Evans & Ben MacIntyre, "NATO Deploys High Tech Weapons", *The Times*, March 29, 1999.
45. Armand J. Chaput, "Design Considerations for Uninhabited Combat Air Vehicles", *Unmanned Systems*, Spring 1998, p. 9.
46. Sara Waddington, "Affordable Lethality", *Unmanned Vehicles*, May 1998, p. 27.
47. Michelson, Op cit., p. 12-13.

48. Malcom R. Davis, "UAVs for the RAN - The Future of the Royal Australian Navy's Fleet Air Arm?", *Asia-Pacific Defence Reporter*, December 1998/January 1999, p. 34.
49. Chaput, Op cit., p. 9.
50. Cdr. Kurt Engel, "Ship Based UAV Systems, Where Art Thou?", *Unmanned Systems*, Winter 1996.
51. Tim Ripley, "The Datalink Challenge", *Unmanned Vehicles*, August 1997; Chaput, Op cit., p. 9.
52. Colin Gray, "RMAs and the Dimensions of Strategy", *Joint Force Quarterly,* Autumn/Winter 1997-1998.
53. *Out of the Sun: Aerospace Doctrine for the Canadian Forces* (Winnipeg: Craig Kelman & Associates, 1998).

Morning Forum

Dr. Joseph Jockel, St Lawrence University

Dr. Nossal, is Kosovo the turning point for the Chrétien Government? Will it now appreciate the role of the Canadian Forces in foreign policy or does this remain a government that is happy to use the military resources that it has on hand but will not change its fundamental thinking regarding the funding for the future of the Armed Forces?

Dr. Kim Nossal, McMaster University

I think that the response of the government and the members of Cabinet to the Kosovo crisis at one level may be a little surprising particularly to those who watched the Liberal Party in opposition in January of 1991 during the parliamentary debate that led to the use of force against Iraq. In particular, very forthright opinions were expressed by Mr. Axworthy in 1991 during his terms as opposition critic for Foreign Affairs. On the other hand, Mr. Axworthy's 'human security' agenda fits so perfectly with the use of force for the maintenance of human rights. To be frank, I do not think that I am that surprised that a minister who does not much like NATO, who does not much like the use of force, would nonetheless see the possibility of the use of force particularly in the context of Kosovo. We have to keep in mind that Mr. Axworthy was the Minister of Foreign Affairs during the genocidal massacre of Tutsis in Rwanda during the 100 days in 1994 and the Serb slaughter of Muslims at Srebrenica in 1995. As a result of both instances, I suggest that he would understand the relevance of the use of force. My position is that you have a much larger obstacle in the way in terms of the budgetary future, that is, the Department of Finance. Let's face it, Mr. Axworthy has fought a large number of battles in Cabinet over budgetary questions and for the most part he has not done very well.

The session was chaired by Dr. Joseph Jockel, Head of Canadian Studies at St Lawrence University in New York State.

Dr. Jockel

General Kinsman, at this moment how would you address the chances, in numbers if you can do so, that the money will be found to upgrade the CF-18 and CP-140 over the next several years?

General Kinsman, Chief of the Air Staff

I will not speculate whether this is a turning point because one of the things we found out in the last number of years, is that to declare a permanent state is fraught with danger. Speaking particularly as an individual who has spent much of his career either in training or fighter aircraft, I think it would be clear to say that after the participation of the CF-18 in the Gulf War, there was a general sense, at least within the fighter community, that the imprint would have been made on the mentality of Canadians and that it would have been very difficult to challenge the requirement for the CF-18. Interestingly enough, it was alluded to earlier, within three years we were not discussing how many aircraft or what capabilities we needed. We were once again discussing whether we needed them at all. Therefore, one can never be sure. I would suggest that the financial condition of the country is now different than it was in 1991-92, so perhaps the participation of CF-18s in Kosovo this time around will have a more lasting impression because the dollar imperatives are not exactly the same. We are not talking about significant budgetary reductions. We are talking at least of a levelled budget. So this is how I would respond to the first part of the question with respect to how optimistic I am about finding funding for the CF-18s and the Aurora. I am actually quite optimistic. It will have an impact, as you do not magically find money to improve aircraft or any other type of weapon systems for that matter without having to take that money from somewhere else. This will translate into activity rates, readiness levels, or the number of aircraft and crews that we are maintaining. It may mean a more varied readiness capability, which always sounds good when you are talking on paper and when there is no imperative to launch a whole bunch of aircraft. But once again, our current exercise shows that you can go very quickly from a modest requirement to something that is much more significant in a very short order. So the military mind always has some sort of trepidation about buying into tier readiness, which minimalizes your current capability to react and respond quickly, as there is always a sense that sooner or later you are going to be called upon to deliver more than that, and people will be disappointed or feel betrayed if you are not able to do that and you will be the person trying to justify why you were in the posture you were. I am confident that we can make do with the current budgetary allocations we have. I am even hopeful that we will be able to shorten that modernisation period. An implementation period of over 8 to 10 years has its problems, but it is better than not having a modernization program at all. So we are hopeful that we will be able to shorten that modernization period.

Khanh Lekim, Chair of the Vietnamese Human Rights Committee

Dr. Nossal, do you think Mr. Lloyd Axworthy's 'soft power' policy is working in Kosovo, and is that a Canadian version of Sun Tzu's Chinese version?

Dr. Nossal

As some of you know, Mr. Axworthy discovered the concept of 'soft power' that was being peddled about in the early 1990s by American academics, most notably Joseph Nye Jr. Mr. Axworthy basically used Nye's notion of soft power as something that the Canadian government could usefully use in its foreign policy. It focussed primarily on the importance of being able to use good ideas to involve negotiations and diplomacy, rather than the so-called 'hard asset', in particular military force, although I think that there are other hard assents that are just as useful from a foreign policy perspective. One of the objections that a number of people, including myself, have to this was that there was a denigration implicit in the conception of soft power; that one did not need hard power anymore. Indeed, if you look at Mr. Axworthy's inclinations, and indeed, if you look at those who are advising him, one can make the argument that there was a general deprecation of military assets, at least by the Minister and his advisers. On the other hand, it is quite clear that from the last week or so, that Axworthy's aversion to the use of military power is in fact quite contextual. In other words, if in general he is uncomfortable with the idea of spending large sums of money to maintain a variety of hard assets, there is no doubt that in particular circumstances he recognizes the importance of the ability to use force. From that point of view, I believe that if he were here, he would probably say that there is no inconsistency between on the one hand advocating the use of soft power for a country like Canada, but on the other hand, in certain circumstances and certainly when faced with the kind of catastrophe that we have seen in Kosovo, hard power is indeed very useful. As the Minister has said, there are limits to negotiations.

Khanh Lekim

LGen Kinsman, I saw a report on the news stating that we cannot send our aircraft overseas since we have to wait until we get assistance from US Air Force for air-to-air refuellers. Do you think that we can overcome this problem? Secondly, can you say a little more about the vision of the Canadian air force for the year 2000?

LGen Kinsman

In response to the question on the air-to-air refuelling capability that we do not have, we ceased operations of the Boeing 707, our strategic air-to-air refuelling capability, a couple of years ago simply because the aircraft was too expensive to operate on a year-to-year basis. Thus we basically gave up temporarily on our ability to deploy CF-18s over long distances accompanied by one air-to-air refueller. However we do have a residual air-to-air refueller capability in Canada with KC-130 Hercules aircraft. They were used in the deployment of some of the aircraft a few weeks ago over to Europe, but they have limitations in their employment, from both the standpoint of range and altitude. Certainly there is an acknowledgement throughout the Canadian Forces that the absence of a strategic air-to-air refueller (similar to the Boeing 707) is a limiting factor in our planning. It does not preclude us from deploying CF-18s. It just makes the deployment of them more problematic, and more dependent on a number of other factors. It is in the not so long-term planning to re-establish an air-to-air refuelling capability, but to be perfectly honest, and this is my personal opinion, I have to focus first on maintaining the combat capability of the aircraft that you are going to use the air-to-air refuelling capability to service and make sure that is guaranteed before I worry about the air-to-air refuelling capability. In an ideal world I would be worrying about the two at the same time, and in fact I am, but my priority is to make sure the CF-18 can fulfil its mandate in the second half of its life.

With respect to a vision for the future, it is the kind of thing that I can ramble on about for some period of time. People taking a look at what Canada's air force will look like for the next 10 or 20 years might argue that it lacks a certain imagination, because it continues in a post-Cold War form and does not seem to be buying into elements of the revolution in military affairs. However I would argue that first of all, our equipment was purchased with a strategy which saw a lot of our combatants being useful for the role, and capable for the roles until somewhere between the years 2015 and 2020. A lot of what we have talked about in the revolution of military affairs is there conceptually; the basic technology is there, the development of technology can be forecast, but many of these things are still on the drawing board. Therefore there is an interim period between now and the time a lot of this actually will become reality.

Stéphane Garneau

Wing Commander Greville, listening to your presentation it seems the Royal Air Force has everything it wants. It is going to up-date, modernize and even go into the new realm of miniature cruise missiles. However, is there a desire for the RAF to become the second leading air power in the world, or at least the leading one in Europe, especially when you have a neighbour like France who thinks they have to assume that role, or are you just trying to keep up to date with current standards for operations, whether it be NATO or United Nations?

Wing Commander Greville, Royal Air Force

I am certainly not aware of any intense rivalry within Europe to try to become the best air force. However, when you start talking to some pilots in various competitions you might find that. In strategic and broad terms, what we are trying to do is to make sure that we remain a well-rounded, medium-sized air force that can fulfill most of the air power roles that are being laid down for us, and certainly within the Strategic Defence Review. In my presentation I discussed quite a large number of new aircraft and missile systems and it is just really felicitous that a lot of these systems and missiles are actually coming into service between the 2000 to 2004. This is a reality because during the late 1980s and 1990s we did not really have any new systems coming into service. We had a really long period of when no new equipment was being received, therefore we started this re-development program and they are all coming to fruition in the very near future.

Dr. Jockel

Wing Commander Greville, how has it been possible for the armed forces in the UK, particularly the RAF, to be able to acquire what (by doing a quick sum in my head) consists of hundreds of millions of pounds? Has there been no political opposition to the expenditure of such a large sum of money on military equipment in the post-Cold War period?

Wing Commander Greville

A lot of things have hinged around the Labour Government coming into power a couple of years ago and their subsequent Strategic Defence Review. I must admit that at the time I thought, along with a lot of my colleagues, "not yet another defence review", because we had undergone so many with the previous government. Most of the previous defence reviews resulted in aircraft being removed from service, including several squadrons, as well as the reduction in our manpower. We thought that the Strategic Defence Review would be the same thing all over again. In reality it has been far from the case. By following a foreign policy review it obviously took a long time to go through the process, but as far as the military is concerned it has been a good result for all three services. It has made us move away from old Cold War thinking to the new era of expeditionary warfare. It has been excellent that the government having made that decision, has decided to put funding in place to give us the money to spend on some of the new systems that we require for this new style of expeditionary warfare.

Roy Thomas

Wing Commander Greville, how many of these projects are going to result in money going into British industry? And how many are going outside of Britain?

Wing Commander Greville

Actually quite a lot of them are heavily involved with British defence and aerospace industries as well as very large consortiums. For example, British Aerospace have gotten together with other European-based defence industries and have moved towards a joint program to develop some of the missiles and the Eurofighter. Therefore, by that stage we decided that the number of aircraft the RAF required in the long-term would be 232, and this figure has not been changed. We are very happy with that result.

The Future of NORAD
BGen Bill Kalbfleish

I will begin my presentation with a quick primer on NORAD for those who might not be *au courant* and also spend a few minutes on the mission of the organization. I will also take a few minutes to talk about the Commander-in Chief NORAD (CINCNORAD) vision, and address some key issues that NORAD will face in the years to come.

As most of you know, since 1958 there have been a series of NORAD agreements varying in length. The most recent agreement was signed in 1996 by Minister Axworthy and US Secretary of State Warren Christopher for a period of five years. Historically, NORAD has been charged with missions of aerospace warning and aerospace control for North America. Aerospace warning includes the monitoring of man-made objects in space and the detection, validation and warning of attacks against North America, whether by aircraft, missiles, or space vehicles. NORAD provides integrated tactical warning and tactical assessment of an aerospace attack against North America, and communicates this information to the national command authorities of Canada and the United States. Aerospace control includes the provision of surveillance and the control of the airspace of Canada and the United States. This in-turn includes the capability to detect, identify, monitor, and if necessary, take appropriate action against man or unmanned air-breathing vehicles approaching North America.

Both the Prime Minister of Canada and the President of the United States have agreed that if both countries are to meet the challenges of the 21st Century we must evolve the institutions that have worked so well in the past, so that they can continue to serve us well in the new millennium. Neither country can best defend North America in isolation. It is with a full bi-national partnership in mind that we engage in the NORAD renewal discussions.

BGen Bill Kalbfleisch is the Vice Commander of the Cheyenne Mountain Operations Centre, NORAD.

The Fundamental Principles of NORAD

Today and in the future, we will be guided by five fundamental principles in NORAD. First and pre-eminent among them is the principle that the defence of our continent is the most basic tenet. Secondly, binational cooperation enhances our defence. Defending our two countries as a whole is both economical and operationally efficient. Thirdly, as a continental defence force, NORAD depends on a total force concept. National Guard and reserve units are a vital components of our everyday mission as well as our search capability. Some of you might not be aware that all of the air defence units in the continental United States are Air National Guard units. Only in Alaska and Canada are regular force units used in a NORAD mission. An Air National Guard option is currently being examined for Alaska. Fourth, due to our sparse units and great geography, logistics are critical to sustain our efforts. For example, we may need to build custom packages of fighters and Airborne Warning and Control Systems (AWACS) aircraft to defend a specific Canadian or US geographic area against the threat of one or a few cruise missiles launched from a freighter at sea. Finally, we believe that credible military threats to our countries will come from the air or space, and not from the land or sea.

The Future of NORAD

Future enemies may not be as deterrable as those in the past. New capabilities are needed to maintain and improve effectiveness. Ballistic and cruise missile defences for North America are likely to be vitally important to our two nations. To that end, I would like to spend a few minutes to elaborate on these issues.

First and foremost, we will need to continue to rely on highly-trained, dedicated, and motivated joint, combined Canadian and US forces personnel. As mentioned earlier, this includes active forces, reserve, and national guard. These are all folks committed to the defence of the continent. It is often seen as a cliché, but we truly believe that our people are our most important component of our command and control system. Our men and women are in the loop at all times in our aerospace warning and control missions. As an aside, in the spirit of jointness from a Canadian perspective, in 1997 it was proposed that the Canadian Army and Navy each man 10 NORAD positions in Colorado Springs. Traditionally, the Canadian Air Force has manned virtually all NORAD positions. Given the future importance of space, the attempt here is to open up NORAD - especially space-related positions - to all three branches of the Canadian Forces. Another initiative has been to increase the number of space-related positions overall in NORAD. Last summer, seven traditionally air defence positions were shifted to billets in the US Space Command. Those positions relate to typical aerospace warning and control activities on behalf of NORAD. This has been done to demonstrate to our US partners our resolve to make meaningful contributions in this area. More importantly, it will help develop higher level of CF expertise in matters relating to space. We are doing this now and hope to reap long-term benefits as we seek more and more opportunities over time.

Matching our people with state-of-the-art technology is also required to face the security challenges of today and in the future. We have heard a little about this from General Kinsman - in particular, the upgrades to the CF-18s. Combined Canadian and American ingenuity and technological know-how can provide NORAD with the required tools to effectively face future security concerns to our shared continent and to improve our current systems to address our areas of weakness.

The NORAD Vision Statement

We have moulded the NORAD vision statement to blend the threat with top-level direction from both Canada and the United States. In particular, the vision responds to both the US Joint Vision 2010 and Canadian defence policy embodied in the 1994 Defence White Paper. We will continue to refine and revise our vision centering on four major areas. These areas depend on and are bound by a strong foundation of information superiority since we are truly an information-intensive command. The four areas are: precision tracking, to detect and track any air or space threat to North America from its origin; precision engagement to deal with threats throughout the full range of our surveillance coverage to ensure off-shore threat engagement; integrated battle-management to provide seamless battle management to fuse information to our NORAD regions and adjacent Commanders-in-Chief (CINCs); focussed logistics to fuse information, logistics, and transportation technologies to support rapid crisis response. All of these would be crucial to providing a credible and effective aerospace defence for North America.

What Are the Threats that We are Concerned About for the Future?

Let me take a couple minutes to discuss three elements of the growing threat that we think could have a great impact on the future of NORAD. These are information operations, cruise missile defence, and Ballistic Missile Defence (BMD).

The first of these is the threat to our information systems. Some refer to this as information operations, or more specifically, computer network attack and computer network defence. It will certainly be no surprise to this audience that information infrastructure touches virtually every aspect of today's society: government, defence, police, industry, finance, transport, electric power, education, to name but a few. This infrastructure is vulnerable to attack and definitely needs protection. The threats includes hackers, organized crime, hostile nations, terrorists, and industrial espionage. We in NORAD are information brokers and we have to deal on a day-to-day basis with high-technology information and communications systems. As you know, we provide warning within a few minutes to the governments of Canada and the United States, so the security and fidelity of the information we use is critical. We need to take the steps necessary to ensure that we protect it and the systems on which it is collected, communicated, and stored. We have a responsibility to do this as a command, but we also offer an avenue through which Canada and the US can collaborate on this on a broader scale in the future. We do not have to go far beyond the most recent experience of the 'Melissa' computer virus to understand just how damaging something as simple as a relatively benign but still quite effective virus was on systems. We ended up closing down our unclassified contact with the outside world for over a week as a result of that virus, so the impact can be quite significant.

The second category of emergent threat to North America is the cruise missile. Today, cruise missiles are widely distributed weapons possessed by over 70 nations. The vast majority of these are short-range naval cruise missiles designed to attack ships rather than land targets. The concern we have with cruise missiles is that as the technology continues to improve their flexibility of use, accuracy, range, and reliability, the threat of their use against land targets grows too. This technology is relatively inexpensive and easily available from a variety of sources. The proliferation even to terrorist organizations is highly likely in the years to come. Their ability to carry a wide range of payloads, from nuclear, to chemical and biological makes them a formidable weapon.

In some ways, though, even more threatening than the cruise missile is the emergent threat possessed by low-observable systems. A low-observable is the name given to a wide array of remotely-piloted vehicles. There are many, many examples on the market today produced in countries around the world. They are inexpensive in comparison to other weapon systems, and some in the intelligence community refer to these low-observables as the 'Saturday Night Special of Cruise Missiles' because, like a cruise missile, they can carry a wide variety of weapons and they are extremely cheap.

That disgruntled nation or terrorist group could fire a cruise missile at North America from a merchant vessel off our coast is a distinct possibility in the future. Obviously, warning, detection, and destruction of such an air-breathing threat is a NORAD responsibility. Much work needs to be done to insure the intelligence is available to warn of this particular threat and on the technology required to detect and destroy them. Today, it is this technology that limits us in our ability to deal with this kind of threat, although there are some encouraging things on the horizon. One example is high frequency surface wave radar, of which we have a couple in Canada. The US Navy is looking in at ways to protect their ships with this radar system which is capable of detecting very low and very small cruise or anti-ship missiles, which would for example increase the ships warning time by a factor of eight times in comparison to the current methods they have available.

The third major threat is that posed by the unprecedented proliferation of ballistic missile technology. This includes programs by countries eager to acquire inter-continental ballistic missile technology with the aid of some of those already in the 'ICBM Club', or those currently seeking to modify shorter range theatre-class ballistic missiles for launching from ships at sea. There is no doubt that many potential adversaries are scrambling for a ballistic missile capability. As many of you know, the US is developing a national missile defence system to provide a capability to defend against limited inter-continental ballistic missile attack. This is not Star Wars or the Strategic Defence Initiative of the 1980s, but rather a program to protect against unauthorized, accidental, or terrorist launch of a small number of warheads. The general rationale in the US is that if the technology to provide the defence is available, it would be totally unacceptable to have even one nuclear detonation from one of these weapons on American soil. If Canada eventually becomes a partner in this activity, it will surely become a NORAD mission.

NORAD Mission 2010

We derived the need for future NORAD missions from our NORAD Mission 2010. Obviously for these new potential missions to become reality, both governments will have to agree on them. The bottom line is our belief that the defence of North America is indivisible. Geographic borders for our integrated tactical warning and attack assessment mission have not been a limiting factor. That mission has a global area of operations and we are convinced that operations in cyberspace even further distances us from strict territorial limitations.

So where do we go from here? Once again, we are embarking on the process of renewing the NORAD agreement for the ninth time in approximately 43 years. The length of each agreement has varied, from as long as 10 years for the first renewal to as short as two years. So there is historical precedence for some latitude in the timing for the renewal of the 1996 agreement. Importantly, the 1996 agreement has a built-in flexibility to allow for expansion of missions if necessary, and at least within that context we can discuss possible additional missions. There is a need to build on past successes and to let the natural evolution of NORAD take place to deal with the threats of the future. As mentioned earlier, we at NORAD are information brokers. Thus information operations are a fact of life that need be dealt with on a daily basis to operate the command. Whether a broader collaboration in this area takes place under the aegis or NORAD or some other bi-national agreement, we believe it does need to happen. NORAD simply provides a convenient avenue, particularly if the US Space Command in Colorado Springs handles the mission for the US. The way to the future points to the use of space as the high ground. We are seeing that daily as part of the events going on in Kosovo and previous to that in the Persian Gulf. To that effect, NORAD is an excellent conduit for bi-national cooperation in space.

On the issue of ballistic missile defence there is a genuine need to educate. We all need to get further into that in order to understand it better. I believe that this is happening in Canada, as I have seen over the internet recent articles in the Canadian media as well as current examination of government policy. Clearly, given its role in the defence of North America should Canada embrace BMD, NORAD would be the logical choice in which to conduct the mission.

Regarding the NORAD agreement renewal, several suggestions have been proposed to the bilateral Permanent Joint Board on Defence by a working group struck to study the renewal options. Proposals range from a full-fledged renewal in 2001 to extending the agreement's duration for 5 - 10 years, or possibly even codifying NORAD in a permanent agreement. There is no perceivable opposition to the 1996 agreement at this time, and it may be acceptable beyond 2001. Whatever the solution, there was consensus that it is never too early to engage in discussion regarding the renewal process, given the major uncertainties that lie ahead and which surround ballistic missile defence. The working group has suggested extending the current agreement for a further five years until 2006. This would appear to be a reasonable approach, recognizing that the decision to deploy BMD would necessitate discussion, possible amendments, or even a completely new agreement, whether that occurs at the five year point or some time earlier.

Conclusion

As NORAD evolves to address several new challenges, our goal will be to continue with the success and relevancy that NORAD has maintained in the past. Space is clearly the key to NORAD providing a credible defence shield over North America. Space systems' continuous availability and global presence permit the precision tracking of hostile air and space vehicles. They can cue conventional forces to precision engagements. They facilitate focused logistics and are crucial to information superiority. This all serves to deter those who have something to lose and to counter those who do not. In the future, NORAD's missions could be expanded to include a limited ballistic missile defence and an effective cruise missile defence. Whether this happens or not, we still believe that there is a bright future ahead for NORAD

The Education of an Air Force: Professional Military education for the Canadian Air Force in the 21st Century
Dr. Allan D. English

Professional Military Education (PME) has become a hotly debated topic in the Canadian Forces (CF) recently, but the armed forces of our neighbours to the south have been vigorously discussing this issue for over two decades. A former Chief of Staff of the United States Air Force (USAF), Michael Dugan, once commented that his air force was producing a generation of illiterate truck drivers. He worried that officers who aspired to senior leadership positions in the USAF knew a great deal about airplanes and tactics but precious little about air power and air strategy. Dugan believed that superior military leaders needed a combination of training, experience, and education to develop the abilities that are required for senior appointments in the air force.[1] A number of commentators have asserted that the need for training and experience has been recognized and addressed reasonably well by western air forces; however, the need for education, especially at senior levels, has not been given the same attention.

The aim of this paper is to discuss briefly how I think the Canadian Air Force might improve its senior officer (majors and above) PME, something that will be crucial in determining its ability as an institution to deal with the complex challenges of the 21st century. I have chosen to speak about senior officer PME because it has been recognized by a number of senior CF leaders, most recently Vice-Admiral G. Garnett, the Vice-Chief of the Defence Staff, in an address to the first National Security Studies Course at the Canadian Forces College, as a bigger problem than junior officer PME.[2]

There is much talk of the value of experience for the professional officer, and there is no doubt that experience is a valuable commodity for

---

Dr. Allan English is a professor of history at the Royal Military College of Canada, Kingston, Ontario.

military leaders to possess. However, as Bismarck pointed out "Fools say they learn by experience. I prefer to profit by other people's experience."[3] Why did he say this? The renowned British military theorist Sir Basil Liddell Hart explained that historical experience is infinitely longer, wider and more varied than individual experience and that history lays the foundations of education by showing how humankind repeats its errors and what those errors are. He went on to say that military history is a good basis for military education because it not only aids in the mental development of the soldier but it also has practical value in teaching the military officer about his or her profession.[4]

In light of Liddell Hart's comments it is instructive to review some of the recent leadership failures in the CF. Professor David Bercuson, a member of the Minister of National Defence's (MND) Monitoring Committee on Change in the CF, recently identified how some of these leadership problems were manifested: 1) a failure to meet increasingly complex and difficult moral and ethical challenges; 2) a failure to maintain the war-fighting ethos which must be at the heart of an armed forces while at the same time conforming to the evolving values of a diverse, educated and rights-driven democracy; 3) a failure to provide consistent leadership of sufficiently high standards and; 4) a failure to be open to both technical and non-technical change. The American armed forces faced this challenge after Vietnam; however, according to Bercuson, it was not a Revolution in Military Affairs (RMA) but a Revolution in Military Education that successfully addressed many of their post-Vietnam challenges. Bercuson says that this solution is a hard one for many in Canada, both in and out of the military, to accept because they see education as a luxury that the CF cannot afford. These people believe that it is easier to convince politicians to buy new hardware than to invest in a better educated officer corps.[5] In a time when other air forces, and other government departments are addressing the challenges of the 21st century by increasing their attention to developing the intellectual capacity of their organizations, I submit that it is time for the Canadian air force to redouble its efforts in this area.[6]

Lessons From History

I would like to look briefly at the period between World Wars I and II for some historical analogies to help guide us, as our predecessors faced many of the same problems that confront us today. At the end of World War I the Royal Air Force (RAF) had 22,171 aircraft and 100 airships in service, manned by 240,00 people. This was quickly reduced to some 200 aircraft and 30,000 personnel.[7] When Sir Hugh Trenchard took over as Chief of the Air Staff in 1919 "there were exactly three officers who had permanent commissions in the Royal Air Force."[8] That was not the end of the cuts, as the 1922-23 budget for the RAF and civil aviation was reduced by 40 percent from the previous year.[9]

Given the precarious state of the RAF, Trenchard's prime goal was to establish a highly trained and efficient air force as a permanent entity. This was to be accomplished by building lasting foundations, such as training schools and colleges, to ensure that the RAF would be able to form its own cadres, and, thereby maintain what he referred to as "an Air Force spirit." The key to inculcating this spirit in senior air force officers and to building the intellectual foundations of the air force, was the RAF Staff College. It was opened at Andover in April of 1922.[10]

In his inaugural address to College staff and students, Trenchard expressed views that would strike a sympathetic chord today:

> Many officers will pass through this College both as instructors and pupils, and in the future from their brains, I hope, will emanate new and brilliant ideas for the development of the Air and its power. I want you to have that one thing perpetually in mind in your studies of the development of the Air. That way lies economy. In my opinion, and it is the only possible opinion, no officer who aspires to a higher position either on Staff or in command can exercise to the full his powers and capabilities if he does not study economy and the power of money to provide what is required.[11]

These remarks show that Trenchard understood well the political and economic imperatives of a peacetime service, but he never lost sight of the fact that he was building a professional fighting force. The RAF Staff College helped to shape RAF thinking during the inter-war years, and it was Trenchard's view that the College would in time become, in what could only be a phrase coined by the often incoherent Trenchard himself, the air force's "cradle of the brain."[12]

The curriculum at the new Staff College was based on the precept that a general education would serve as a sound foundation for the creation of a school of thought in the RAF. And the College's first Commandant, H.R.M. Brooke-Popham, declared that the course of study aimed to develop "the habit of steady reading and thinking rather than... the acquisition of a mass of detail." Good advice for today's PME as well.

Another key purpose of the RAF Staff College, Trenchard declared, was to analyze past war experience and to devise new principles of air warfare and new doctrine to guide the RAF in the future. Trenchard hoped that this would remedy what he saw as a serious deficiency in the new RAF, namely that it had "the experience of war in many theatres to guide us, although it has not been committed to paper in any readily accessible form." This problem was addressed partially by publishing and distributing each year throughout the RAF a selection of the best essays and lectures given at the Staff College by means of an official publication until it was superseded by the Staff College journal *The Hawk* in 1928.[14]

Despite the progress resulting from Trenchard's initiatives, the RAF's doctrine of strategic bombing that evolved during the 1920s was divorced from the reality of the time. The RAF of 1928 consisted mainly of wooden biplanes with limited ranges and capabilities. Its main operational experience was derived from aerial policing duties - dubbed "Air Control" - which gave the RAF a rationale for its existence but did little to prepare it for a war between industrial states. However, its problems were exacerbated by its own tendency to downplay genuine analytical thinking about air warfare and to tolerate a wide gulf between rhetoric and reality almost until the beginning of World War II.[15] A future CAS and one who was involved in making the RAF's inter-war doctrine, Sir John Slessor, declared that RAF inter-war doctrine was largely "a matter of faith."[16]

The other major air force in the English-speaking world suffered cuts similar to the RAF after World War I. By war's end there were over 16,000 flyers in the United States Army Air Corps (USAAC), but rapid initial cuts were followed by further force reductions until by the Depression its strength averaged 1,500 officers and 15,000 enlisted men. In addition, its budget was cut from about $27 million in the late 1920s to $3.5 million in 1938.[17]

After World War I the US Army continued to see its Air Service as an auxiliary arm, but eventually two schools of thought emerged in the USAAC: a "tactical" and a "strategic" school, and some claim both still exist in today's USAF. The War Department, dominated by ground combat arms officers, issued the first Air Corps doctrine publication in 1926 and it reflected the "tactical" point of view. It declared that the air forces' main role was "to aid ground forces to gain decisive success." This was the *official* doctrine of Army aviation from 1926-40. However, a competing "strategic" outlook eventually developed at the Air Corps Tactical School (ACTS), originally set up at Langley Field, Virginia in February 1920. Most of the men at ACTS were disciples of the controversial air power theorist "Billy" Mitchell. They were seen as radicals by the rest of Army, and when ACTS moved from Virginia to Maxwell Field, Alabama in 1931, they set out consciously to become centre for air power thought.[18]

According to Tami Davis Biddle, ACTS developed an "American way" of thinking about air power which it invested with national pride and loyalty, and those who accepted it became tenaciously committed to it. The staff at ACTS consolidated the thinking of the school into an essentially unwritten operational doctrine articulating strategic attack as a war-winning weapon. The heart of this doctrine was precision, high-altitude, daylight strategic bombardment, even if it was not technically possible at the time.[19] But ACTS taught its doctrine for so long that it was widely understood and accepted throughout the Air Corps by 1941. However, according to James Mowbray, ACTS doctrine was produced in the same "ad hoc" manner the USAF has used to write its doctrine ever since.[20] As with the RAF in the inter-war period, the USAAC was committed to its way of war - daylight precision bombing - more as a matter of faith than of knowledge arrived at empirically, and the absence of data left a void to be filled by speculation and extrapolation.[21]

As we have seen, the two primary institutions for air force PME in the English-speaking world in the inter-war years had a number of features in common. They both had the purpose of being the centre of their respective air force's school of thought and both came to be recognized as a centre for thinking about air power. Both had influence (to different degrees) on their air forces' doctrine, and both produced an air force officer corps imbued with common ideas about how to fight air warfare. Finally, both turned out reasonably well-prepared (by the standards of the day[22]) staff officers who were able to rise to the challenge of leading the largest air forces the world had ever seen. However, neither produced a critical analysis of the problems of air warfare in the inter-war years, and relied instead on their faith in an appealing but untested way of waging war.

Requirement For the 21st Century Officer

Today and in the foreseeable future, the conduct of warfare and operations other than war is, and will remain, an increasingly complex activity which requires careful analysis to ensure that it is carried out effectively and achieves the goals set by the government. A number of different commentators have suggested that the essential competencies for the 21st century senior military leader are strong analytical, conceptual, and communications skills, tolerance of ambiguity, intellectual flexibility, and an ability to exploit the chaos of war.[23] The key to instilling these competencies through PME is to ensure that leaders are able to develop new ways of thinking about things, not just to learn new facts. Many believe that thinking innovatively could be our greatest force multiplier.[24]

At a conference at Banff in the fall 1998, leaders in higher education, business, and government recognized that Canadian leaders in the next century, whether civilian or military, will need to think of creative solutions for the new problems that will arise, and because technically-based training can soon become obsolete, the knowledge-based requirements of the next millennium will place a higher premium on creative thinking than technical expertise. The conference participants agreed that a liberal arts education, because it is not an end in itself but a means to achieve improved critical thought, better writing and speaking skills, and the promotion of flexibility, was an excellent way to achieve these goals.[25]

These are very similar attributes to the ones identified in 1995 by General Richard Chilcoat, former commandant of the US Army War College, as being necessary for senior leaders in the armed forces of the 21st century. He described them as follows: impeccable communications skills; the ability to derive lessons from history; the capacity to exercise peer and cross-cultural leadership; and the capability to innovate, to use mental flexibility in critical thinking and in dealing with conflicting information and apparently paradoxical situations.[26] The required competencies listed above are in fact the competencies found in most professions. Therefore, I would like to examine briefly the question "what is a military professional?" in the context of this paper.

General Charles E. Wilhelm, Commander-in-Chief of the US Southern Command, described US military officers of the 1960s as trades people, proficient in the technicalities of war but uneducated in the social context which must invariably shape the US military. The difference between trades people and professionals is that trades persons or technicians use tools without a comprehensive knowledge of how those tools came to be, whereas a professional, because of his/her understanding of how and why the tools were made, is able to adapt the tools for new uses in innovative ways or to modify them to meet unforeseen requirements.[27] If being a professional is so vital to the effective practice of the profession of arms, what exactly does it mean to be a military professional?

One of the best explanations of officership as a profession was given by the distinguished American scholar Samuel Huntington.[28] He explains that the three defining characteristics of a profession are: expertise, responsibility, and corporateness. Expertise is specialized knowledge acquired only by prolonged education and experience. Essential to maintaining this expertise is continual study and practice of the profession. The professional also has a responsibility to practice his/her profession in the service of society; the profession therefore holds certain moral principles in dealing with laypersons. Finally, professionals share a sense of unity among themselves and separateness from those who are not members of their profession partly because of the lengthy training necessary to achieve professional competence.

The military profession lays claim to the expertise of the application of violence by a military force in the service of the state. The duties of officers include: 1) the organizing, equipping, and training of this force; 2) the planning of its activities; and 3) the direction of its operation in and out of combat. As Huntington points out, modern military forces contain many types of specialists. However, only those who "manage violence" are true military professionals. Others, such as doctors, dentists, lawyers, pharmacists, etc, may have expertise that is necessary for the military force to achieve its objectives, but they are not competent to manage violence. As Huntington puts it, they belong to the officer corps in an administrative capacity, but are not part of the professional body of the officer corps. Most specialists are trained in professional schools (eg., medical schools) and serve only a small part of their career in the military, usually returning to practice their profession in a civilian setting.

If one accepts the definition of a profession presented above, it might be disturbing to read a recent article in *Vanguard* magazine titled "Renewing DND's Culture: Lessons for the Way Ahead." In it the author, John Moore of PricewaterhouseCoopers, a leading accounting and management consulting firm, described current cultural change initiatives in the Department of National Defence (DND) that he had been hired to implement almost entirely in terms of a civilian company. While no one would disagree with some of Moore's "desirable features of a renewed DND culture," for example, "Teaming" or "getting people to work together in extremely efficient ways" is no doubt desirable, but for an organization whose primary function is the application of force in the service of the state, I would not describe the desired outcome of "Teaming" as the generation of "a high quality service or product."[29] Surely we can do better.

Most disturbing to me was Moore's approach to basics and re-committing the Department to its core values. It is a good concept in theory, but Moore suggests that this can best be achieved by adopting state-of-the-art management tools and techniques, and among other ways, by targeting "intact work teams that tend to work together to execute business processes" and by using "real business issues facing the team." This is the type of advice one would expect from a businessman, someone who follows different *métier* from the military professional, but I would hope that "renewing DND's culture" would be more about integrating the core values of the profession of arms into the Department than dealing with business issues.

Armed forces will always need the advice of experts from other disciplines, including business people, and I think air forces have regularly been tempted by the methods of other professions because air forces rely heavily on technology and the advice of specialists in using the latest technology. But in the end they must focus on their primary purpose - preparing to employ violence in the service of the society.

How We Are Doing Today

Now that military professionalism has been defined, the next section of this paper is a brief examination of how successful the CF has been in achieving it. According to David Bercuson, formal education is the touchstone of professionalism because it can sharpen critical skills so the military professional is able to make effective decisions and to understand the human context of war today. The MND has directed that, beginning in 1997, a university degree would be a prerequisite to commissioning as an officer in the CF, except for those commissioned from the ranks.[30] The latest figures on formal education in the CF officer corps compared to the American officer corps are that about 50 percent of Canadian officers have a university degree compared to almost all American officers, and that 10 percent of the Canadian officer corps has a postgraduate degree compared to about 50 percent of American officers.[31] A conference of leading Canadian educators and military officers charged with education and training in the CF held in December 1998 at the Royal Military College of Canada (RMC) concluded that the reason for this discrepancy was the lack of a clear policy supporting the MND's direction. And more specifically they said that there was no policy framework in place to define selection for education, to support education and to address the career implications for those pursuing formal education. Conference participants noted that "[t]he CF does not manage individual careers well," and that higher education often ends up being a "career punishment."[32]

It is perhaps worth pointing out here that the Canadian military is not alone in having problems with PME. A conference on the subject hosted by the US Naval Postgraduate School and the Office of Naval Research in January 1998 identified serious problems with the American PME system. A preliminary analysis of the conference findings concluded that the current American "officer career development systems are seriously flawed" because they do not allow enough time for officers to complete all the requirements for operational and command experience, joint duty, post-graduate degrees, PME, and staff assignments expected of them. In addition it claimed that the American PME program was "seriously under-funded and over-stretched."[33]

Those attending the Canadian conference at RMC proposed these solutions for CF problems. Career management must involve: the identification of those with the ability to profit from post-graduate studies and the nurturing of that talent; the selection of appropriate personnel, and; the effective utilization of the graduate to get maximum return from the investment for the CF. These seem like simple measures to take, but according to the conference report the CF is not able to implement them because the Assistant Deputy Minister (Human Resources-Military) maintains overall responsibility for officer education and professional development in CF but that the three environmental services pay for advanced education. To rectify this situation, David Bercuson suggested that a single budget structure for advanced education was needed in the CF.[34]

There may be a need for a single education budget and more comprehensive education policies in the CF, but I would suggest that even if these are implemented (and certainly until they are implemented), the Canadian Air Force needs to take steps to oversee its own PME and the subset of the profession of arms that is found in the practice of air warfare.

The Way Ahead - Some Possible Solutions

This section presents a few potential solutions to what the Canadian Air Force can do in the short term to improve its PME at minimal cost. First of all, I suggest the air force devise policies to ensure that PME rooted in the profession of arms is given to its officers, particularly senior officers.

One must be proactive in this regard and not just assume that any graduate degree will provide the requisite PME based on the profession of arms. The figures cited earlier that about 50 percent of American officers have post-graduate degrees can be misleading, as it turns out that most of these degrees are MBAs and similar "second career" degrees (degrees designed to prepare people for other professions or occupations after their military careers).

As Colonel Dennis Drew, currently a professor and associate dean at the USAF's School of Advanced Airpower Studies and a former faculty member at the Air University put it: "the Air Force is in the paradoxical position of putting a high value on graduate-level education that is largely irrelevant to its *raison d'être*. The Air Force seems unable or unwilling to distinguish between the value of a graduate degree in business from the value of a graduate degree in national security studies or military history."[35] According to Drew the outcome of this situation was that most USAF officers (80-90 percent of the officers who attended the Air Command and Staff Course and 50-60 percent of the officers who attended the Air War College) were "appallingly ignorant of the bedrock foundation of airpower thinking, virtually oblivious to airpower theory and its development and without any appreciation of airpower history and its meaning."[36]

The Canadian situation, as I see it, has some similarities to the USAF circumstances. It is my observation that most people pursuing post-graduate education in the Canadian air force are doing so because of their own initiative. They are, almost without exception, excellent students. But little has been done to make their post-graduate education more relevant to their military careers. I think we need to focus these students more closely on areas of study directly relevant to the profession of arms. In some cases this might mean insisting that the institutions we are funding (directly or indirectly) offer these types of courses on a regular basis. Furthermore, we must insist that sponsored candidates (and encourage unsponsored candidates) to take the majority of their courses in areas directly related to warfare, especially air warfare. How can we do this?

My second suggestion relates to this issue and the issue of encouraging PME. For me, the key lies in consistently rewarding personal professional development. This will require a comprehensive plan to select, educate, and employ those who have the potential to become the air force's senior leaders of the future. It may require the creation of institutions like the USAF's School of Advanced Airpower Studies, but as a minimum I believe that the air force needs to have a place to focus its thinking about air warfare. This leads to my third suggestion.

In order to help the Canadian Air Force face the challenges of the future, a Canadian centre of airpower studies is required to be able to study all aspects of air warfare, up to the highest levels of war in a joint context. I believe that the best way to accomplish this goal is with the creation of an Air Warfare Study Centre. (I use the term "Air Warfare" here because I believe it should study all aspects of atmospheric warfare, including topics related to surface-based systems, not just those topics that are often more narrowly related to the employment of aircraft usually subsumed under the heading "airpower.") An Air Warfare Study Centre could co-ordinate the study of air warfare in Canada; advise the Air Staff on the education and employment those who have the potential to become the air force's future senior leaders; collect and study the current and past air warfare experience of Canada and other nations; publish the results of this analysis; provide the theories and principles of air warfare upon which sound doctrine can be written; and employ some of those senior air force officers who have the education, experience and aptitude to do the tasks described here.

Conclusion

Michael Howard has aptly summarized the problem that armed forces, including air forces, will face in the future: "I am tempted to declare dogmatically that whatever doctrine the Armed Forces are working on now, they have got it wrong. I am also tempted to declare that it does not matter that they have got it wrong. What does matter is their capacity to get it right quickly when the moment arrives."[37] Vice-Admiral Garnett gave our first NSSC a similar message. He said that we need to

> Guard against current and past successes creating complacency about changes required for the future. What the Canadian Forces do well now is no rigid formula for our success in the future. Different circumstances often require different solutions. Our current strengths in some areas may only be transitory in value. The future may well demand other kinds of forces with other kinds of capabilities.[38]

We have seen that, to deal with these issues, future leaders will, among other things, need to be able to think critically and analytically, tolerate ambiguity and exploit the chaos of war, and posess intellectual flexibility.

Finally, no matter how pervasive technology becomes in war, victory or defeat will still depend on the ability of the military leader. Or as the distinguished Canadian historian, Donald Schurman, put it in an RCAF Staff College journal article published 35 years ago: "The proper commander's most valuable qualities will not be determined by his specialist training, but by his reflective intelligence, his moral strength, and his quality of will."[39] The challenge for those of us who are concerned about "the education of an air force" is to help the senior leaders of the air force in the 21st century develop these attributes.

Notes

1. Dennis M. Drew, "Educating Air Force officers: Observations after 20 years at Air University," *Airpower Journal* 11, no. 2 (Summer 1997) [citations from online version at <http://132.60.140.12/airchronicles/apj/sum97/sum97.html>], 1.
2. "Speaking Notes for Vice-Admiral Garnett, Vice-Chief of the Defence Staff, " The National Security Studies Course, Toronto, Ontario, January 6, 1999, <http://www.dnd.ca/eng/archive/speeches/nssc_s_e.htm>.
3. Cited in B.H. Liddell Hart, *Why Don't We Learn from History?* (New York: Hawthorn Books, 1971), p. 15.
4. Ibid., p. 15, 16, 18-9.
5. D. J. Bercuson, "Defence Education for 2000...and Beyond," in "Educating Canada's Military: Workshop Report, December 7-8, 1998," Kingston, ON: Royal Military College of Canada, p. 25-6.
6. For example, the Department of Foreign Affairs, Industry, and Trade has set up its own think-tank and has given many of its better minds a chance to brainstorm. Hugh Winsor, "Axworthy Flourishes in Role of Busybody," *Globe and Mail*, March ,1999, p. A4.
7. Phillip Meilinger, "Trenchard and 'Morale Bombing': The Evolution of Royal
8. Air Force Doctrine Before World War II," *Journal of Military History* 60 (April 1996), p. 251.
8. Andrew Boyle, *Trenchard* (London: Collins, 1962), p. 541-2.
9. Denis Richards, *Portal of Hungerford* (London: Heinemann, 1977), p. 79.
10. Allan D. English, "The RAF Staff College and the Evolution of British Strategic Bombing Policy 1922-29," *Journal of Strategic Studies* 16, (September 1993), p. 409-10.
11. Air Marshal Sir H.M. Trenchard in Ibid., p. 409.
12. Neil Young, "British Home Air Defence Planning in the 1920s," *Journal of Strategic Studies* 11 (1988), p. 507.
13. English, p. 410.
14. Ibid., p. 411.
15. Tami Davis Biddle, "British and American Approaches to Strategic Bombing: Their Origins and Implementation in the World War II Combined Bomber Offensive," *Journal of Strategic Studies* 18 (1995), p. 101, 105. For example, it was not until March 1938 with the first meeting of the Bombing Policy Sub-Committee of the Bombing Policy Committee that the RAF did any real thinking about the operational issues of how to get bombs on target, p. 114.
16. Cited in English, p. 427.
17. Mark A. Clodfelter, "Molding Airpower Convictions," in *Paths of Heaven*, Phillip S. Meilinger, ed. (Maxwell, AL: Air University Press, 1997), p. 105.

18. James A. Mowbray, "Air Force Doctrine Problems 1926-Present." *Airpower Journal* (Winter 1995), p. 23-4.
19. Davis Biddle, p. 112.
20. Mowbray, 25-6.
21. Davis Biddle, p. 114, 127.
22. To put in perspective the fact that virtually no one who completed the courses at the RAF Staff College or ACTS had a university degree, we should remember that even at the end of World War II barely seven percent of Canadians had attended a post-secondary educational institution of any kind, Bercuson, p. 27.
23. Walter F. Ulmer, "Military Leadership into the 21st Century: Another 'Bridge Too Far?'" *Parameters* 28, no. 1 (Spring 1998), p. 4-25; and A. Okros, "Strategic Human Resource Analysis," presentation given at the Royal Military College of Canada, March 24, 1999.
24. Steven H. Kenney, A Professional Military Education and the Emerging Revolution in Military Affairs,@ Airpower Journal 10, no. 3 (Fall 1996), p. 52.
25. Nancy Dorrance, "Liberal Arts: Irrelevant or Irreplaceable?" *Queen's Alumni Review* 73, no. 2 (Mar-Apr 1999), p. 6; and Bill Leggett, "The Case for a 'Broadly Based' Education," *Queen's Alumni Review* 73, no. 2 (Mar-Apr 1999), p. 7.
26. Richard A. Chilcoat,"Strategic Art: The New Discipline for 21st Century Leaders," (10 October 1995), <**http://www.dtic.mil/doctrine/jel/ research_pubs.htm**>, from the Joint Electronic Library of the US Joint Doctrine web site, p. 12, 16, 17, 22.
27. Bercuson, p. 27, 30.
28. Samuel P. Huntington, "Officership as a Profession," in *War, Morality, and the Military Profession*, Malham M. Wakin, ed. (Boulder, CO: Westview Press, 1986), p. 23-34. The theoretical concepts in this paper are based on Huntington's essay.
29. John Moore, "Renewing DND's Culture: Lessons for the Way Ahead," *Vanguard* 4, no. 3 (nd, [1999?]), p. 10-12.
30. Bercuson, p. 23, 26.
31. A.J. Barrett, "Foreward," in "Educating Canada's Military: Workshop Report, 7-8 December 1998," Kingston, ON: Royal Military College of Canada, p. iii.
32. "Educating Canada's Military: Workshop Report, 7-8 December 1998," Kingston, ON: Royal Military College of Canada, p. v, 11, 23, 28.
33. "Preliminary Summary Analysis of the Conference on Professional Military Education sponsored by the Naval Postgraduate School and the Office of Naval Research," at <http://web.nps.navy.mil/FutureWarrior/Analysis. html>, p. 3, 4.

34. "Educating Canada's Military," p. 11, 14, 29-30.
35. Drew, p. 3-4.
36. Ibid., 1, statistics from note 1, p. 8.
37. Sir Michael Howard, "Military Science in the Age of Peace," *JRUSI* (March 1974), p. 3-4.
38. "Speaking Notes for Vice-Admiral Garnett."
39. D.M. Schurman, "Science and Military Decisions," *Air Force College Journal* (Toronto: RCAF Staff College, 1964), p. 42.

The Canadian Aerospace Defence Industrial Base
LGen (Retd) Dave O'Blenis

The interface between the Canadian military establishment and industry is very important and extremely complex. It is worthy of in-depth consideration. However, this has not happened, except in some parts of what used to be in Industry Canada and International Trade. This morning's presentation on the Revolution of Military Affairs suggests, and I follow USAF General Chuck Horner's forays into this area, that the RMA is very much connected to technology, industry, and the interface on the procurement side.

I would recommend to anyone who is interested in this relationship between the military and industry in Canada the minutes of the Standing Committee on National Defence and Veterans Affairs (SCONDVA) meetings of late March 1999 on acquisition reform. The Canadian Defence Industry Association (CDIA) appeared before the committee. Some of the questions asked by the Committee were very interesting because they were either very naïve, or they revealed a significant understanding of the situation, as the committee members asked questions to which there are really no answers.

What is this military-industrial relationship? My experience in this area is not vast from either side, but since retiring from the air force I have worked with several industry-related organizations. I was the Vice-Chair of the Canadian NATO Industrial Armaments Group (NIAG). This group is essentially the national armaments director's interface with the industry in Canada. I am now the Vice-President of the Canadian Defence Industry Association and I try to work with industry and the Department of National Defence primarily. I also work with other government departments. I am also on the Board of Directors of the Aerospace Industries Association of Canada (AIAC), which is working on this issue

---

LGen (Retd) David O'Blenis is Vice President of Business Development and Governmental Affairs for AlliedSignal Aerospace Canada.

as well.

Traditionally, our federal government has grouped aerospace and defence together under Industry Canada. This has not been really satisfactory from the aerospace companies' perspective, as they would prefer to talk about high technology and how it relates to government policy, and do not want anything to do with defence. From the defence perspective it is also unsatisfactory as the defence industry is left out of the loop. The view of the Canadian Defence Industry Association is that defence business is good business since it involve high technology and thus has many spin-offs.

AlliedSignal is a fairly large company. Last year's sales were $25-billion worldwide. Approximately $15-billion was in aerospace (Bendix, Air Research, Garret, Homing are some subsidiaries). Eighty percent of AlliedSignal's aerospace business is commercial, the rest is military. Thus 20 per cent of $15-billion is $3-billion. AlliedSignal has approximately 71,000 employees and we have increased our sales by 50 per cent. Therefore I can identify with what General Kinsman was saying about doing more with less.

The aerospace industry is very cyclical. It has been growing since 1995, but we are now at the top of the cycle, and we are moving downward. Boeing, our largest customer, will be producing 630 airplanes this year. This number will decrease in the following years.

The industry is currently undergoing a period of consolidation, similar to what you see in the military. In Canada the aerospace industry accounts for $400-million annually.

I am currently involved with two missile programs which employ approximately 1,500 people in Toronto. One program is an air-to-air missile, led by BGT in Germany. It is a very high-performance dogfight missile. We are just in the engineering development stage, and we are delivering the first hardware for trials on the CF-18s. After the trial period we will move to low-rate initial production.

The second missile is the Evolved Sea Sparrow Missile (ESSM). Six nations are involved in this project, including Canada, and 13 nations have shown interest in buying the product. We have had some successful firings and we are now in the early stages of low-rate initial production. The control actuation centres for both missiles were built in Toronto.

A Short History of the Canadian Aerospace Industry

The aerospace industry in Canada began before the First World War in support of exploration activities in northern Canada. During the Second World War the industry expanded to support the war effort. Even rail car manufactures converted to aerospace companies. One example is Victory Aircraft, later known as Canadair. It built 10,000 airplanes in Canada during the Second World War.

After the war, the aerospace industry moved to a more commercial base venture. The real break from defence productions occurred when the famed CF-105 Arrow was cancelled, as it did away with a total military aerospace capability in Canada. In the agreements that followed the cancellation, Canada agreed to acquire major American systems, and in turn the US agreed to buy Canadian components without any tariffs. Thus began Canada's preferred trading partnership with the US in aerospace technology.

During the last 15 years there has been rapid growth in the non-defence aerospace industry in Canada, with the exception of a brief decline during the recessionary period between 1991 to 1993. In terms of world ranking, Canada has the fifth-largest aerospace industry, which had total sales of $15-billion in 1998. However this total accounts for less than four per cent of the world's production capability. The Canadian industry is highly export-oriented and approximately 80% of the sales are commercial. It currently employs 67,000 people.

Canadian aerospace companies are world leaders in selected niche markets. The principal markets include regional and business aircraft (Bombardier), commercial helicopters (Bell Helicopter Textron), small and medium turbine engines (Pratt & Whitney Canada Inc.), landing gear systems (Menasco Aerospace), and aircraft environmental systems (AlliedSignal Aerospace Canada). Other significant niches include flight simulators and visual systems, power management and generation systems, and last but not least, space robotics (Spar Aerospace Ltd).

Growth in Canada has been quite spectacular, but it has been leveraged by what we call a 'Snow White'. There are three Snow Whites - Bombardier, Bell Helicopter Textron, and Pratt & Whitney Canada Inc. The rest of the aerospace companies are all dwarfs by comparison. The three Snow Whites have sales of over $1-billion each and Bombardier alone had over $3-billion in sales last year. In turn, the dwarf companies average approximately $500-million in sales per year.

The sales of Canadian aerospace goods in 1998 are classified into six markets. The biggest category by a significant margin is airframes, which accounts for 48% of sales. The second largest market is propulsion equipment, accounting for 22% of sales. Defence electronics accounted for nine per cent, while avionics and space accounted for eight per cent and four per cent respectively. All other markets accounted for nine per cent of sales in 1998.

Exports account for the vast majority of sales. In 1987, 37% of the sales were to domestic customers, while 63% were to foreign buyers. By 1998, the percentage of foreign sales had risen significantly. Last year, foreign buyers accounted for 78% of total sales. The vast majority of exports consisted of airframes from Bombardier and deHavilland, and to some extend the engines from Pratt & Whitney. It is expected that the margin between foreign and domestic sales will continue to increase.

The vast majority of our foreign sales are to the United States. However, the percentage has decreased in the last decade or so. In 1985, 75% of our foreign sales were to the US. Thirteen years later, in 1998, only 60% of exports went to the United States. The US is still a major market, however its dominance continues to shrink. Thus in the next few years the proportion of sales to other nations will continue to rise.

In terms of sales by region in Canada, Quebec continues to be the aerospace capital of Canada. Ontario is second.

Today, the biggest customer of Canadian aerospace technology are the major civilian users such as airline companies. Bombardier's sale of aircraft to airlines had a significant impact on the increased percentage to this market. Airline companies and other users account for 56% of products bought in 1998, a significant increase from the 1985 total of 38%. In comparison, governments, both Canadian and foreign, account for only 18% of purchases of aerospace products, a decrease of 12% since 1985. Aerospace and defence manufacturers purchased 27% of aerospace material in 1998, a decrease of 11% in comparison to the 1985 figures.

Now let's look at the sales to military and civilian markets. In 1980, 40% of all sales were to the military market, however this number has been reduced by 50% in less than 20 years. Since 1984 there has been a very slow growth rate in sales to military markets while there has been a substantial growth in civilian markets. In 1984, sales to military markets accounted for approximately $1-billion. Sales to the civilian market were approximately $2-billion. In 1998, sales to military markets were approximately $4-billion, while the sales to civilian markets were 3 times larger, approximately $12-billion. It is expected that this discrepancy will continue to rise in favour of the civilian market.

With regard to sales, the real question we must ask is how much we actually contribute to the final product, known as value-added (percentage of Canadian content). A great example is Bombardier's Global Express airplane. Some components for the wing are built in Quebec, then shipped to the Far East where they are assembled, flown back to Canada and placed on the airplane. Traditionally, Canadian aerospace is a very high valued-added industry. However, the current trend is negative as Canadian content continues to decline since smaller Canadian aerospace companies are being squeezed very tightly as a result of globalization. Thus in order to continue to be competitive, principal Canadian aerospace companies such as Bombardier are being forced to source certain productions offshore. This is very worrisome from the point of view of the employment of a specialized workforce. Since 1997, many Canadian aerospace and defence companies have been sold, consolidated, or changed names. This process continues as we speak. This mirrors trends in the global aerospace industry.

The heritage of the Canadian defence industrial base began with the removal of US tariffs after 1959. There has been more or less a balance in defence trade between both nations, although some of the offsets in Canada have been commercial rather than military. The majority of major systems are sourced in the US whenever possible. The Canadian industry's equal opportunity to compete for US Department of Defense contracts has also had an important impact, since Canadian firms have access to this significant American market. The US Department of Defense has also enjoyed this equal opportunity program as they have a greater source of supplies and base to work from. However, I believe that this is disappearing.

Issues

The Defence Production Sharing Agreement and the Defence Development Sharing Agreement between Canada and the US have essentially lost their teeth because of developments in world trade, World Trade Organization rules (WTO), the lack of funding sources to support the development of new products and technologies in Canada, and the cancellation of the Defence Industry Productivity Program (DIPP) by the Liberal government in 1993. It was replaced by Technology Partnership Canada (TPC). However, the TPC is the only source of shared risk investment in Canada as there are almost no Canadian defence research and development contracts. These currently total only $200-million compared to $60-billion in the US.

The Defence Production Sharing Agreements (DPAR) and the International Traffic in Arms Regulations (ITAR) are being amended by US State Department. This will eliminate approximately 60% of all repair and overhaul of-US built military equipment done in Canada, since we will not be able to obtain the data to bid for the packages to do the work. It is kind of ironic that even US-based companies cannot obtain this data in Canada. It is all in the name of protecting secrets, but in reality it is in the name of protectionism, or non-tariff barriers. This dispute is currently going on between our two governments. This is very disturbing in terms of the Canada-US relationship.

Globalization has had an impact. Aerospace is definitely a global industry. Foreign ownership is accelerating in Canada. According to a survey conducted by the Canadian Defence Industry Association, 58% of contracts over $1-million went to foreign-owned Canadian companies such as AlliedSignal. It is really a global supply base. Our small and medium aerospace enterprises in Canada have to be world class in order to compete, and it seems, with a few exceptions, that there is always someone out there who can do it as good or even better at a cheaper cost. As a result, Canadian companies are losing contracts. Therefore Canadian companies must become more competitive.

Afternoon Forum

Dr. Jockel

BGen Kalbfleisch, it is quite possible that NORAD might be coming to an end if the Canadian government does not agree to participate in National Missile Defence (NMD). Have you given any preliminary thoughts on how to structure Canadian-US aerospace cooperation without a joint command?

BGen Kalbfleisch

This is an interesting observation. Certainly, without National Missile Defence (you have to make the assumption that it will go forward) it will definitely create some practical difficulties for NORAD. Activities performed by Canadians in Colorado Springs in the integrated tactical warning and attack assessment in the Space Control Centre could become areas that we might not longer be able to work in. I do not know if that means that the defence of North America as a bi-national activity would go away. I am speaking from a personal perspective because I am not sure that anybody has really delved terribly deeply into this point since the federal government has not made a decision. There had been proposals as a result of the Quadrenial Defence Review to re-align the defence of North America by creating an Americas command. Whether this might surface and move some of the more traditional NORAD activities away from US Space Command is one possibility. There is no doubt that much of what you say is possible but I think it is a little early yet to raise the white flag.

LGen (Retd) David O'Blenis

Obviously there has been some discussion of this in Canada.

The session was chaired by MGen (Retd) Fraser Holman, a member of the CISS Board of Directors.

Bob Morton and Brian Smith are two Canadians who have thought of this possibility. Their conclusion is that there are ways to restructure the agreement if Canada is not involved in National Missile Defence. Initially this might work, but in the long term it would become irrelevant, as would Canadian participation.

Dr. Kim Nossal, McMaster University

This is the first time I have heard a Canadian official present in public a justification for the transformation of NORAD. It seems to me that your justification - the notion that North America is under threat from missiles, from space, from low-observables - would not make an impression on the Canadian public. I believe that if the government were to make this presentation to the general public, they would say that this does not makes a lot of sense. Would it not be better to level with Canadians in the following sense: that the Americans are extremely concerned about this threat? We (the Canadian government) do not actually believe that Toronto, Montreal, or even New York are actually going to be hit by rogue states, since no rogue state would like to invite a response from the US. But we as Canadians think that their concerns are at least reasonable enough that it would be appropriate and prudent to go through with a National Missile Defence system. I worry that if the government tries to run this campaign in Canada, using terms that are simply borrowed from the American debate, it will create more political opposition in Canada than if the government would basically lay it out as an American problem to which Canadians, as we have been for the last fifty years or so, are ultimately sympathetic.

BGen Kabfleisch

These are some excellent points. I do not disagree with what you say. Nevertheless we look at it from a bi-national perspective. We either have a bi-national institution as we have and until now, or it will have to change. I am not sure that if we use the approach that you suggested that it would get any additional impetus for support. It is being the nice guy "let's help them out" type of approach. I guess that the heart of the matter lies in whether there is a credible threat. That is a hard question to answer. We see things that are going on, we see activities that some countries are involved with, and that leads us to believe that this threat is evolving.

The other element is the accidental launch of a weapon. This is not the launch of a weapon by a rogue state or terrorist, but rather the result of some accident or incident. Can we convince the Canadian public that its appropriate to invest in some form of insurance against that capability or against that potential situation given the number of systems that are primed to go? I honestly do not know. There are policy issues that will be difficult to come to terms with, especially trying to convince the Canadian public that a real threat is out there. But if one goes back 10 years, we could not have for seen all the things which have transpired. Does this enter into the question? This debate is also going on in the US. We will have to see how the decision unfolds if a decision to deploy is made. I agree that there is going to be some difficulty on both sides of the argument due to the investments that will be required.

Khanh Lekim

BGen Kabfleisch, now we are talking about a revised SDI program. Can you tell me some facts and justification why we need the kind of system?

BGen Kabfleisch

As I mentioned, the concern is the proliferation of ballistic weapons. If you look at the last decade or so you will see that the Cold War is over, START II is facing some difficulties in being ratified, and there are many weapons still out there. The possibility of accidents, or misjudgements are present. In addition, Russia faces difficulties with its early warning as many of its satellites are no longer active due to their financial constraints. Therefore the potential exist for Russia to react inappropriately to a foreign launch of a rocket or missile. A great example is the rocket launch from Norway that created a great deal of angst in Russia in 1995. There is an uncertainty there.

The proliferation of ballistic missile technology elsewhere is also a great concern. I do not disagree with the comments from Dr. Nossal concerning which country is going to go ahead and do something knowing that great havoc will be wreaked upon them immediately in retaliation. Those are the deterrent actors. What about the 'undeterables' and the terrorists. Where is this leading? These are very valid questions that you ask. These are issues that are trying to be addressed in the US, and to determine how this threat will evolve in the next 10 years or so. If the perception is that the threat is real, I believe that the government will make the decision to go ahead. Obviously, given the billions in investment that will be required, if there is some sense that the threat is too low, I believe that we can anticipate non-deployment. But that is a tough one to call right now, and the feasibility of such a system and the possible threats are still being studied.

LGen (Retd) O'Blenis

National Missile Defence is not SDI. This is a very limited capability and it has no capability against major arsenals, including those of China and Russia. What we are talking about is an insurance policy. When you buy insurance you do not know what will happen in the future. I do not get the problem except for cost, which is a US decision. It is only part of a whole piece, which is largely information brokerage. NORAD and US Space Command are brokering information which is unavailable from any other source in realtime. The problems the Russians have right now is that they are losing that information since they can not afford it.

Khanh Lekim

Mr. O'Blenis, can you tell me more about Canada's role in the new international space station, including the new version of the Canadarm.

LGen (Retd) O'Blenis

The technology for the Canadarm was developed with investments from the Canadian government. The intellectual property resides in Canada. It cannot be exported and that technology will play a large part in making the space station work. Other Canadian companies are also involved in the new international space station. AlliedSignal is currently making some environmental control systems, and we are also working on a system to develop power for the station. We are working with the Canadian Space Agency to develop a flywheel energy storage system, which operates on magnetic bearings. Hopefully this might also produce energy to stabilize the station. It has a lot of applicability to low-orbiting satellites.

Stéphane Gremeau

Mr. O'Blenis, you stated during your presentation that the aerospace industry is under-funded for research and that it should get more funds from the government, especially to assist in the development and survival of this industry. Don't you think that the government's subsidizes this industry to the point that their survival depends on grants?

Without federal grants, should the industry not cut its profits or re-invest them properly? I get the feeling from reading newspapers that every time there is a recession aerospace companies threaten to close down their plants and cut jobs if they do not get their grants and/or tax breaks. Thus why do they ask for more research money?

LGen (Retd) O'Blenis

This is a very good question and one that has been significantly misrepresented in the press in terms of what is really going on in the global aerospace industry. Most nations consider aerospace a critical industry, part of the nation's wealth in terms of technology and growth. As a result, all G-7 nations invest public money in the industry. In the US, that is largely done through the Department of Defense - approximately $60-billion per year - most of which goes into the aerospace sector. In the UK, Prime Minister Tony Blair announced 350-million pounds sterling of grants to the aerospace industry and promised to do better next year. In France and Germany, many of the aerospace companies are government-owned, which do not need to make a profit and thus can make a strategic decision to invest in technology.

The performance of the Canadian aerospace industry is incredible given the fact that we have had so little government investment to balance the playing field between our principal competitors. Defence Industry Productivity (DIP) which was supposed to be defence based became very much commercially based. In fact, the money you are talking about came mostly out of DIP. I think the utopia should be no government investment in aerospace industry world-wide, thus letting the industry compete. But if you are in a country like Canada, and you see what is going around you, the message has to be to the Minister of Industry John Manley, if you see this as a strategic importance to Canada, then something has to be done to allow us to compete globally, especially against those heavily subsidized by governments.

In general, the reality is that it is there, and if you want to develop aerospace technology and create 67,000 jobs, investment is required. Investment is a national security exemption. I am optimistic that Canada will continue to compete, notwithstanding the fact that the underbelly of the industry seems to be threatened.

Student

Dr. English, the air force is the youngest service, and it has experienced continuous technological change. To what extent can you reasonably expect professional officers to stay abreast of their own service? As an outsider I consider them, culturally, to be optimistic to a fault. This might be difficult to overcome. Do you think that there is an interest within the air force in learning from the past rather than just honouring its traditions?

Dr. Allan English, RMC

I would not want to be dogmatic and say that the air force is an institution that is totally technologically-driven, but Dr. Howliet accused the United States Air Force of having technology drive its doctrine. I believe that there is a certain amount of this that goes on. In Canada, Dr. Jack Granatstein remarked that the problem with the Canadian Armed Forces, not just the air force, is that RMC was essentially an engineering university producing engineering graduates which approached everything with a technological mindset. I guess to a certain extent this has characterized our military culture. However, I have seen a lot of sympathy for the other point of view which is to try to refocus on the profession of arms. What I have seen happening at the Staff College gives me a great deal of optimism that there is a recognition of the need of a core of knowledge based around the profession of arms that will still be able to address the technical questions. The focus should now be on the profession of arms rather than technology alone.

Grant Dawson, doctoral candidate, Carleton University

Dr. English, you mentioned in your presentation some discouraging statistics regarding the graduate and post-graduate degrees in the Canadian Armed Forces in comparison to the United States. Could you comment on these contemporary statistics with reference to the Royal Air Force? And if the stats are higher than the RAF could you comment on whether or not it is due to the Trenchard legacy?

Dr. English

First of all, I do not have any stats for the Royal Air Force. Now let me fall back on my personal experience. I was on exchange with the Royal Air Force for three years at the Air Navigation School between 1978-1981. I believe that out of a staff of approximately 100 officers, there were maybe four with university degrees: the Education Officer, two RAF Officers, and myself. It was quite normal for the RAF to take people out of the equivalent of high school and run them through their aircrew training and aircrew career, and they might at some point bring them back for higher studies. They thought that we were quite strange in insisting that people go to RMC or a civilian university to get a degree before they went flying. They often referred to the fact that the Canadian system was trying to educate and train people and then try to motivate them enough to stay in the service as a career. The RAF claimed that by giving people education later on in their career, they were training the motivated. You can argue the point either way.

Quite frankly, I do not know which system is better. I think a strong case can be made, especially in view of aircrew retention problems, of taking people right out of high school and running them through career training, and during their nine-year contract, putting them through continuing education to earn a degree, or if you they really good, sending them off to earn a degree. But I would suggest that at the senior officer level - major and above - we should be seriously looking at a minimum of a bachelor's degree, and hopefully at some point, with service assistance and funds, a post-graduate degree.

Closing Remarks
Don McNamara

Ladies and gentleman, it is my privilege and pleasure as a former air force officer, former member of the directing staff of Canadian Forces College, Honourary Colonel of the College, and as the past President of the Canadian Institute of Strategic Studies, to have the opportunity to have the last word at what has been an outstanding opportunity to discuss air power and its implications for Canada.

It is very important that we try to understand where we have been today, starting with this morning when Mr. Rudd said that the impact of air power is pervasive in our everyday lives. There is probably no single person in this room within the last few days that has not felt some impact of air power, whether it is watching television, been on an aircraft, or in some way been involved directly in the operation of aircraft. It is really important that we gain an understanding of this in the broadest sense and try to bring that understanding to the wider Canadian community.

General Kinsman talked about Canada's air force. He looked at today's air force in terms of missions and vision. He talked about the fundamental principles including rapid response, technological upgrades, and inter-operability. He also looked at the future. In addressing the Revolution in Military Affairs (RMA), he underlined some of the real issues including cost constraints and inter-operability requirements. He pointed out the essentials for the future Canadian Air Force: decisive leadership, to be able to modernize and embrace RMA selectively, to be able to maintain global deployability and responsiveness, to maintain inter-operability, to provide effective stewardship, and to participate in valuable partnerships. This is a pretty tall order, and it links up with some of the things that Dr. English subsequently mentioned regarding the need for education, since only the best officers will be able to achieve those lofty goals.

We then heard from Kim Nossal, who has been engaged in a private and public confrontation with the Minister of Foreign Affairs and International Trade over the nature of 'soft power', its utility/disutility,

---

BGen (Retd) Don McNamara is the Past President of the CISS.

and how exposed it is when it is without any kind of hard power back-up. Dr. Nossal stated that air power is a key instrument of both domestic and foreign policy. He addressed this issue through a number of dimensions, and pointed out that our future strategic environment appears very much like the past: that our post-Cold War period will be dominated by the United States, and that Canadians should ensure that they are able to understand and are capable of supporting the US in these ventures. He also mentioned that we have to make sure the US is involved in world affairs, and to avoid isolationism by either the US or Canada. Often it is said that we contribute as little as we can get away with in regards to national interest, but we must make sure that whatever we contribute is appropriate to maintaining that national interest. During his closing comments, Dr. Nossal stated that the real isolationists in Canada are in the Department of Finance, and a shrinking capability overall has a profound influence and effect on our foreign policy.

We were then treated to a very interesting overview of the current and future capabilities of the Royal Air Force by Wing Commander Greville. He described in great detail the various aircraft and other systems coming into service in the RAF; a result of a very objective and particularly effective Strategic Defence Review done in Britain. The Strategic Defence Review is a bottom-up analysis of what a country needs for its defence. The effectiveness of that analysis is proven by the quality of the programs that the RAF is pursuing in response to the government's analysis.

Before lunch we had a interesting presentation on Air Power and the Revolution in Military Affairs by Dr. Paul Mitchell. There are a number of major issues that were discussed. One of the highlights was the need for a fundamental re-assessment of the role of Canada's air force, particularly in this new strategic environment. In the context of the RMA, I would also suggest and recommend to you *Adelphi Paper 318*, "The Revolution in Strategic Affairs", by Lawrence Freedman. In both the *Adelphi Paper* and Paul's concluding remarks, it was pointed out that only the US can afford the systems involving the total RMA, but that this very fact might drive conflict into different kinds of relationships, with non-state actors doing an end-run around their state adversaries. There is no way that they could confront the US and its systems head-on, therefore you end up with other asymmetric threats which include, as stated by Lawrence Freedman, "The bomb in the paper bag in the shopping mall." The challenge the governments will face is how do you address on the one hand the overwhelming capability that technology may be able to provide, but on the other hand the overwhelming response which is almost unmanageable by those who are prepared to react.

After lunch General Kalbfleisch posed a number of questions about current and future NORAD operations. I will not try to reproduce his comments except to say that. There is a real need for assessment and re-assessment of Canada's role in NORAD and to recognize the current threats which range from information operations on the one hand to cruise missiles, low-observables, and the ballistic missiles on the other. According to some reports, 70 countries have some ballistic and cruise missile technology. That, out of a world that has about 185 countries, represents a substantial proportion of countries that could represent a potential threat to our well-being. The NORAD renewal is an extremely important element of Canada's future security and is one which I believe, as was discussed here, not well understood by the average Canadian. As Kim Nossal noted, how do you sell this to the average Canadian? I believe that through workshops such as this and through the missionary effort that will arise from being exposed to these questions, we will realize that we must communicate with the Canadian public at large and provoke informed discussion on this very important issue. This is true not only in regards to ballistic missile defence but also the whole military relationship we will be having with the United States in the future, because it is of fundamental importance to Canada's national security.

Dr. Allan English had a very interesting presentation on the education of the air force officer. I am absolutely mystified as to why there has been this sudden emphasis on executive MBA programs except to provide an easy and very expensive retirement for some officers. When Bill Weston and I were in this classroom here together some 28 years ago, the course we received at the CFC was a military MBA. That is the way we should be looking at the kind of education we should provide. We should not think for a minute that university MBA programs are going to provide anything for the military that the military cannot provide for itself. The challenge for air force officer education, both at the undergraduate and graduate level, is going to be extremely important to the other element that we talked about a moment ago - dealing with the NORAD renewal issue and communicating with our political masters. So the real value of this education process is going to be providing the most effective senior air force officers with the communications skills and the knowledge base absolutely necessary to communicate most effectively with the Canadian public and with political decision-makers. And without that, the air force will not even get to first base.

Finally, David O'Blenis' presentation gave us a very interesting overview of the aerospace and defence sector. He identified a number of problems, not the least which is the decline of government subsidies, as well as the role and nature of the Canadian aerospace and defence industry base. As he pointed out, we have the fifth-largest aerospace industry in the world, but it represents only one percent of the world overall in terms of doing business. These are important figures to keep in our minds.

In the course of our morning and afternoon fora, we had some excellent questions and discussions. I would like to thank all of you for having been here to contribute to that discussion and also for being here to provide an audience for the presenters. I would also like to thank all those who have helped to put this together. We have some great volunteers including Maureen Smith, Brenda Yates, Deyan Kostosky, André Beauregard who is an intern with the CISS, and of course David Rudd, the Executive Director, and Jim Hanson, our Associate Executive Director. I must also thank our two moderators, Dr. Jockel and Fraser Holman. On your behalf I would like to extend our thanks to them for contributing to a first-class seminar.

THE CHANGING FACE OF WAR

Major Dave Mason, Wing-Commander Sean Bell,
Major Jeff Boucher, Major Kwang-Sun Jung,
Major Dave Oickle, Major Rick Pitre,
Major Brad Smith, and Major Chris Whitecross

"Victory smiles upon those who anticipate changes in the character of war, not upon those who wait to adapt themselves after the changes occur."[1]   Guilio Douhet, 1921

Introduction

A great deal has been written about the likely changes in the nature of war in the first two decades of 21st century. Changes in the geopolitical make-up of the globe in the decade following the end of the Cold War, combined with the continuing exponential growth and application of technology, are having an ever-increasing impact on the conduct of warfare. Air power, traditionally the most significant benefactor of new technologies and a major element in operations across the entire spectrum of conflict, stands on the brink of a new millennium, poised for the doctrinal changes and challenges that await.

It may be argued that over the past century, the conduct of warfare has transitioned from one of attrition to manoeuvre, facilitated largely by this technological change and the application of operational art. However, the harsh reality of warfare has come under closer scrutiny in the public forum and significant pressure has been brought to bear on the military to 'sanitize' this brutality. As described by Richard Hallion in a recent *Joint Force Quarterly* article, "... characteristic of modern post-Gulf, post-Somalia military operations: to win quickly, decisively, and with remarkably few casualties..."[2]. This has become the typical civilian populace mindset as they no longer have the propensity to accept long, ambiguous, and costly conflicts.

We are now confronted with the question of how the application of air power will evolve in the face of these new realities. This essay will examine the changing nature of war in the first two decades of the 21st century, focussing on two main themes: global geopolitical transformation, and the impact of the revolution in military affairs (RMA). In order to set the stage for this examination, we will also analyse potential threats within the international security environment over the next 20 years. These elements will be examined with regard to their effects on the application of air power, focussing on the roles, missions, and equipment that may characterise air power in the near future. Finally, we will discuss the changing nature of air power from a Canadian context and provide recommendations as to how the Canadian Air Force might cope with these changes.

International Security Environment: 2000-2020

A review of relevant Canadian and allied security assessments indicates that there is general consensus about the international security environment during the next twenty years. While the Cold War was notable for its relative simplicity and predictability, the next twenty years will be characterised as dynamic, uncertain, and complex. A number of trends will influence the geopolitical environment, among these the emergence of multiple centres of power, a weakening of the "state", and globalisation. These trends will be further impacted by ethnic, economic, social, demographic, and environmental strains, leading to increased instability and the potential for violence, conflict and war.

In addition, a number of combat functions will develop and mature over the next twenty years that will have an impact on the nature of conflict.[3] Foremost amongst these is the proliferation of weapons of mass destruction (WMD) and the means to deliver them. The advancements in conventional weapons and the emergence of information warfare also promise to significantly impact the nature of conflict. These new weapons and war-fighting capabilities will serve to asymmetrically threaten the major powers.

The potential for conflict between states will remain one of the main security threats. While the United States will likely remain the pre-eminent power, the emergence of multiple centres of power will complicate the international security environment. Russia, China and India will likely compete with the US, and amongst themselves, for influence. In addition, a number of other powers - North Korea, Iraq, and Iran for example - will also vie for regional dominance. It is reasonable to assume that at least one regional power will resort to large-scale military aggression against its neighbours. The likely availability of weapons of mass destruction will further complicate the situation.

In addition to the risk of large-scale inter-state conflict is the increasing incidence of failed or failing states with the resultant instability, internal conflict and humanitarian crises.

This security environment is further complicated by trans-national threats such as terrorism, organised crime and the illicit drug trade, all of which are likely to become more dangerous and pervasive in the new millennium. Other potential trans-national threats include natural disasters (with their attendant recovery and refugee problems) and environmental catastrophes.

In the decade since the end of the Cold War, direct threats to North America were considered significantly reduced. However, over the next 20 years these threats are likely to resurface. Russia and China will maintain their ability to directly target North America with WMD while other emerging regional powers will likely develop this capability. Terrorism, the threatened use of WMD by trans-national groups, and information warfare also serve to directly threaten North America.

In developing a coherent and effective national security and defence policy, and shaping the CF to support it, it is essential that a comprehensive assessment of the threat and how that threat has changed since 1989 be conducted. The "peace dividend" has not materialized. Indeed, while the Cold War permitted the luxury of primarily focussing on one adversary (the Warsaw Pact), threats are now developing from a plethora of areas which threaten Canadian vital interests, both directly and indirectly. Developing an effective national security policy to counter these threats will be a key contributing factor to Canadian security over the next twenty years.

Changing Nature of Conflict in the 21st Century

Given the wide spectrum of possible conflict scenarios attracting the attention of the world's militaries, tailoring forces and doctrine for the next 20 years will be a challenging task. The familiarity of the Cold War, with its attendant opportunities for training and preparation in an evolutionary manner, enabled doctrine, weapons systems and training to be modelled on a relatively small number of possible conflict scenarios. Training was focussed on providing a rapid response to the Soviet threat and a capability to provide support to UN-sponsored peacekeeping efforts. Weapons were developed and procured for a particular theatre, tailored to contain and destroy particular equipment with relatively little regard for collateral damage. In this era, quantity was at least as important as quality. However, in the new world security environment, forces must train and prepare for the unknown. They must be prepared to deploy for significant periods of each year, and often into areas that do not necessarily afford training opportunities for forces to maintain readiness in the full spectrum of military skills. Weapons must be "surgical" in nature, they must limit collateral damage, and they must be used in limited numbers to avoid adverse publicity under close scrutiny of the media, or so as not to provide opportunity for exploitation by enemy propaganda. Furthermore, militaries must be cognizant of the political demands on the military in the case of atypical contingencies requiring military assistance, such as disaster relief or aid to the civil power.

Conflict Challenges

As the global distribution of power changes, the political influence and ambitions of nations and state actors is refined. For example, the World Bank anticipates that China will have the world's largest economy by 2025, but does not project the impact this may have on that nation's ambitions in the world arena.[4] On a smaller scale, the new security environment will likely expose new threats from states that are less susceptible to the logical cost/benefit accounting of the Cold War deterrence theory, thus presenting a new challenge for the more traditional defence doctrine of the military. Regardless of the nature of the threat emerging over the next two decades, it appears likely that military forces will have to be prepared for a broad spectrum of operations, be flexible and responsive, and be well trained and equipped to cope with a wide variety of possible contingencies. Notwithstanding the difficulties associated with establishing the precise nature and dimensions of any future threat, certain trends have emerged in the prosecution of defence doctrine which should enable forces to prepare for the challenges that lie ahead.

Current conflict models may not be flexible or sufficiently adaptable for the militaries of the next century. For example, the strategic instrument of choice for a given campaign or conflict theatre is likely to be theatre-dependant; based on imagination and initiative rather than established doctrine. A future Gulf War scenario would likely result in air power being the strategic instrument of choice, particularly if there was limited requirement for ground forces to take or secure land, with other military arms being used to support the lead effort. However, in jungle warfare, a terrorist-based threat or a liberation/intervention operation, the relative merits of the individual service contributions may be very different. Notwithstanding this caveat, technological advances have directly influenced air power's capabilities, ensuring it remains a potent and credible consideration for the future.

Force Structure

Increasing budgetary demands and shifting national priorities vis-à-vis defence and social programmes will continue to focus military attention on how best to exploit limited resources while still providing a credible and capable force. Forward-basing is expensive, increasingly vulnerable and, in the absence of an easily identifiable adversary, is unlikely to provide suitable forces in the right place at the right time. In addition, the increasing demands of operational deployments on service personnel favours home basing to provide an element of stability for families. However, the natural corollary of this premise is that forces must maintain a high degree of readiness and be able to deploy at short notice (with a degree of autonomy) to almost any theatre in the world, regardless of available host nation support. To ensure credibility, these forces must not be bound by Cold War doctrine; rather, they should be well trained, adaptable, flexible, and able to apply initiative and leadership in a professional and efficient manner. Inasmuch as these deployed forces may be required to make the ultimate sacrifice, they must be suitably equipped and protected to limit unnecessary vulnerability and optimise confidence in equipment and training. They must also be sustainable - a factor recognised most effectively in one of the core themes of the US military's "Joint Vision 2010". Finally, strong support from the political leadership will be fundamental to the success of these forces, particularly in the increasingly sensitive and conflict-adverse world likely to prevail in the future.

Impact of the Revolution in Military Affairs (RMA)

One of the key tenets of the much-vaunted Revolution in Military Affairs (RMA) is the increased accessibility of information and the associated requirement to filter, interpret and control the information arena. Indeed, the management of information, both in accessing and interpreting, provides a unique and distinct challenge to the military of the future, as the ability to operate within the enemy's decision cycle is still considered crucial to success on the future battlefield. An effective decision can only be made based on valid and timely information, so control and processing of information is a key element of the RMA and indeed in the successful prosecution of Operational Art. In future conflicts, the flow of information necessary for the successful prosecution of the campaign is likely to be voluminous and of varying degrees of accuracy, so suitably trained personnel will be vital to the efficient management of this element of the forces. Furthermore, and with few exceptions, future conflicts are likely to be prosecuted in concert with allies, in a coalition force or at least with external assistance. Accordingly, the ability to operate within an integrated force, in a joint environment, will be crucial to the success and credibility of any future contribution to a military campaign. In short, the key to maintaining a high operational tempo will not necessarily be sortie generation, but the ability to reduce the time spent in the command decision cycle. Interoperability with key allies and the ability to collect, process and interpret information and deny the same opportunities to the enemy, will be key factors in the successful prosecution of military campaigns of the future.

National Choices

The aspirations outlined above are ambitious, and probably fall outside the technological or budgetary constraints of most sub-superpower nations. Accordingly, most other nations will be obliged to conform to US standards of equipment and interoperability. The extent and nature of conformity with the US model will probably be directly related to the political influence sought, and thus there will be little motivation for developing an independent capability in deference to the alternative strategy offered under "big brother" cover. A degree of specialisation in the information arena may offer individual nations the opportunity to offer a tailored "golf club" to the "golf bag" spectrum of military requirements. However, the likelihood of any superpower relinquishing an element of total information dominance to provide any nation with a unique niche specialisation, and thus independence, would appear unlikely at this stage.

At some stage during the next 20 years, select militaries will have the ability to find, fix, track, and fight anything on the earth. However, a nation's ability to maintain a comprehensive military technological advantage is likely to be increasingly difficult to achieve, primarily as a result of financial restrictions. Potential adversaries with a specialist capability, tailored specifically towards a perceived weakness in the conventional capability of friendly forces, would present a significant threat to any future campaign. If Iraq had procured SA-18 surface-to-air missiles prior to the Gulf conflict, the nature of the campaign could have been very different. In addition, the rate of technological advance is ever-increasing and to be fully exploited, procurement systems must be far more responsive and mid-life updates must be tailored accordingly in order to maintain a technological advantage over any potential adversary.

Reducing costs associated with access to space may also shift greater emphasis to the military's role in space control in military operations. Emerging "cutting-edge" technology is usually expensive, and a truly comprehensive capability will be beyond the reach of most, if not all, national players. Furthermore, the employment of future weapons are likely to be heavily influenced by the media together with the political and public expectations, both realistic and ideal, of the military's capability and accountability. In addition, in the future, civilian casualties may be interpreted as murder, especially if "dumb", or unguided, weapons are used in preference to a precision option. Usage of non-lethal weapons may redefine what is considered "acceptable" conduct in limited warfare. Development of such weapons may render participation in any conflict that might result in significant casualties unsupportable and thus, unsustainable and prone to failure. Stealth technology appears to be the decisive element at this stage; however, any technological advance offering stealth detection may render this technology obsolete overnight, leaving some very expensive technology sidelined from future campaigns.[6]

Public Perception

Despite the wide range of conflicts being conducted all over the world, the number attracting sufficient attention to merit intervention by Western governments is relatively small. Furthermore, individual national involvement in a number of potential conflict scenarios will be determined largely by political motivation, which will in turn be driven by a variety of factors. The decision to commit military forces will be influenced by the capability and track-record of the forces concerned, together with the political imperatives of the moment. Regardless of motivation, political concerns will likely be focussed on the vulnerability of any dedicated force to casualties, and on their capacity to limit collateral damage and civilian casualties. The media is likely to be most influential in this regard, so planning for the future must include the involvement of Public Relations and the education of the media to help ensure realistic expectations of the outcome of any conflict. The Gulf War and the ensuing media coverage has probably convinced the public and political leadership that precision weapons can be used with impunity, and will always be the most suitable and appropriate option. However, the conflicts of the future are unlikely to follow any established template; indeed, future protagonists are likely to have learned many lessons from the numerous tactical and strategic errors of Iraq's military leadership, and new strategy and tactics will undoubtedly be required in the future. The public and political leaders must be made aware that conflict usually involves significant sacrifice in lives, on both sides, and that the limited casualties of the Gulf War may be the exception rather than the rule. The danger of ignorance in this regard is that political or public support for future operations may be very fragile and may ultimately undermine the strategic aims and effort.

Application of Technology

The uncertainty surrounding the scope and scale of potential future conflicts requires a pragmatic but innovative approach to defence planning. As Stephen Biddle illustrates, in Operation DESERT STORM, the vast majority of equipment employed was 1960s and 1970s technology; however, this does not explain why the Iraqi losses were so great and those of the US-led coalition so low.[7] Despite the relative merits of technology available to the Iraqi leadership, no technology can make up for errors in making or implementing strategy. To be effective, the military, political and industrial structures must offer synergy, imagination and initiative to provide the force multipliers inherent in the new and emerging technology. Technology, by itself, may have limited effect on the battlefield without effective organisational infrastructure, and the successful application and utilisation of emerging technology will form a further interpretation of operational art. With the boundaries between the strategic, operational and tactical levels of war becoming increasingly transparent, technology increases the importance of strategic vision and the vital application of operational art. The synergy of organisational ability, the human element and technology provide the basis for truly robust and credible military superiority.

The truly effective military force must increasingly rely on well-trained and motivated personnel in order to capitalise and optimise the synergy of technology and organisation. They also provide the best hedge against the uncertainties of the world ahead. People represent the heart of any professional military capability, and quality will generally prevail against quantity, when applied in concert with technology and political motivation. However, as military organisations throughout the Western world face reduced budgets, downsizing, and an uncertain future, attracting, recruiting and retaining quality personnel will be a major challenge for the next century. Quality-of-life initiatives, improved career prospects, quality training and increased responsibility will all help ensure that this most valuable commodity remains as effective, credible and well-motivated as possible. The Gulf conflict demonstrated the limited potential of a well-equipped adversary with poorly trained or motivated personnel, and the conflict in Vietnam served to demonstrate the tenacity and effectiveness of a well-motivated and dedicated force, despite its limited technological capability in equipment or information management. The lesson, as illustrated in Joint Vision 2010, is clear: people are the foundation, and their training, well-being and motivation are paramount in ensuring that armed forces are capable of adapting to the changing security environment of the future.

Impact on Roles, Missions and Equipment of Air Forces

The next logical step in determining the impact of the changing face of war on air power calls for an examination of the roles, missions and equipment required to combat the emerging threats of the next century. Fundamental to this effort is the need for allied air forces to develop strategies and programs that are compatible with one another and that are financially viable.[8] While not all nations will be able to afford the full range of programs, it is necessary to examine each in careful detail. The United States military is, conceivably, the only military force capable of operating autonomously in every part of the spectrum from Operations Other Than War (OOTW) to full-scale combat, including nuclear war. However, it has recognized that such a capability comes at a cost. Technology, shrinking budgets, and the changing nature of warfare manifested by new threats, has brought about a revolution in military affairs (RMA).[9]

Core Competencies

In an effort to meet these new challenges, the United States has recognized the need to identify essential core competencies for its air force. The six core competencies determined to be critical in support of future United States national security strategy are Air and Space Superiority, Global Attack, Rapid Global Mobility, Precision Engagement, Information Superiority and Agile Combat Support.[10] What makes these factors unique is the notion that all are geared towards engaging in regional conflicts far from the shores of North America. It has, however, become apparent that the United States is increasingly unlikely to fight alone. While it remains the only force capable of independent action, it requires the credible support of its allies as a means of engendering legitimacy for its actions. To ensure the provision of an effective contribution to a coalition, allied nations should choose core competencies they can both afford and apply as credible force multipliers.

Roles

It is also useful to examine the six core competencies in terms of the functions and roles they each perform. Listed below are the functions normally associated with Western air force doctrine:[11]

Counter air	Counter space	Counter surface
Counter sea	Strategic attack	Counter information
Airlift	Air refueling	Space lift
Intelligence	Surveillance	Reconnaissance
Combat SAR	Weather Services	Command and Control
Special Operations Forces		
Navigation and Positioning		

As stated earlier, it is important to understand that no nation, aside from the United States, will have the capacity to provide combat-ready forces to execute all of the above mentioned roles. It would be reasonable therefore, for nations to identify their Air Force roles based on an assessment of their nation's priority for air power - for example, sovereignty and missile defense. However, these roles must not only be chosen to satisfy their domestic concerns, but must also complement the overall coalition effort in a theatre of operations. In the analogy of the golfbag, each nation would inevitably supply a different club to the golf bag.

Equipment

Air power today and in the future will offer the advantage of reach, concentration, and the flexibility to conduct multiple operations over a wide area. As technology develops and new platforms and capabilities emerge, the relevance of air power will become even more apparent. New technologies will permit air forces to detect, localize, classify and destroy or disable targets with pinpoint accuracy. One has simply to study the evolution of data collection methods from the days when scouts were dispatched on foot or by balloon to gather information, to today's application of high-tech reconnaissance aircraft, Unmanned Aerial Vehicles (UAV) and space-borne assets to project where the future might lie.

Questions arise as to how traditional functions may evolve given advances in technology and the need to guarantee less risk to human life. While the pilot-less cockpit may appear attractive, there will be certain functions that still demand the presence of a human pilot. For instance, air-to-air refueling and troop-transport, which invariably involve human cargo will, in all probability, continue to be manned by human operators. The roles of intelligence, reconnaissance, surveillance, and EW aircraft may, in all likelihood, be the first to succumb to the pressures of automation.

While human costs associated with combat continue to drive automation efforts, one has also to consider the material costs of large and expensive platforms used to carry human occupants. Assets such as the Combat Talon, AWACS, JSTARS, and Rivet Joint are critical to any operation and the loss of any one or all of them could severely alter the course of a campaign. Human and material costs have sparked interest in developing platforms that are much smaller, more versatile, automated and less expensive.

Interoperability

As mentioned to earlier, air forces of the future will be increasingly dependent on their ability to operate and communicate as a part of a joint, combined or coalition force.[12] The emphasis therefore must be placed on interoperability in order to provide effective air power. This can only be accommodated with commonality of communication systems, training, standards and doctrine. A sustained ability in Information Operations (IO) is also essential for interoperability.

Common language code and transmission formats are essential as more players access command and control nets to obtain vital information. Interoperability will continue to plague those nations unable to afford the information systems needed to access critical data.[13] NATO and the UN are two prime examples of organizations that continue to struggle with interoperability problems. Standardization in areas such as equipment and materiel compatibility may never occur but these tend to be in areas that become logistical problems rather than operational ones. However, NATO does seem to be interoperable in the critical areas such as communications, command and control, and common operating procedures. It is unrealistic to believe that complete commonality is achievable given the vast number of players involved. Furthermore, countries may be reluctant to share sensitive technologies and information-gathering techniques if they possess a significant advantage in these areas.

The major changes in roles, missions and equipment will impact the way command, control, communications and intelligence (C3I) is conducted. The migration of these functions to space-based assets, unmanned aerial vehicles and more efficient manned aircraft means that information will arrive in greater volume, at higher speeds, and with startling accuracy and resolution. Commanders will have access to the most detailed information needed to plan and execute an operation. The next challenge they will face will be how to filter and process this information to a form that is readily useable and available on demand. Information operations will continue to be prominent in the conduct of future air force operations. Success, to a large extent, will depend on how well future air forces can tailor their roles, missions, and equipment to combat the threats in the twenty-first century.

The Canadian Air Force in the 21ST Century

Defence Priorities

Certain assumptions can be drawn regarding Canada's position and the ways in which it can effectively cope with the changing nature of warfare. First and foremost is the assumption that foreign policy objectives will, in all likelihood, remain relatively constant. Canada has a long-standing tradition of internationalism and therefore will continue to pursue "Pearsonian" policies. Similarly, defence policy will continue to serve both domestic and foreign policy objectives. What will differ, however, is the approach and prioritization of defence objectives within the defence policy framework. Defence objectives will continue to focus on preserving and protecting the sovereignty of Canada, remaining committed to the defence of North America within a formalized defence arrangement with the United States, the continuance of the contribution to international peace and security, and finally the traditional roles of Assistance to Civil Authorities (ACA) and Aid to Civil Power (ACP).[14] In essence, the objectives outlined in the current Defence Planning Guidance should not change dramatically over the next twenty years.

The Missile Threat

As mentioned earlier, one area of major concern is the proliferation of WMD. The widespread black marketeering of WMD will continue as cash-starved nations illegally exchange technologies and hardware for hard currency. Unconventional or asymmetrical threats from rogue actors will pose the greatest danger both to Canada and other nations. Ballistic missile defence (BMD) will become increasingly more important in deterring threats to national sovereignty. As this nervousness peaks, the globe may witness an increased reluctance on the part of Anti-Ballistic Missile (ABM) signatories to honour commitments in keeping with de-nuclearization ideals. Canada will have to contend with this issue in the near future as the United States continues to forge ahead on Ballistic missile defence (BMD) initiatives. Canada's position on BMD, while idealistic and certainly characteristic of her nature as a champion of the Nuclear Non-proliferation Treaty (NPT), may very well have to be re-examined to reflect the current state of world affairs. Some may suggest that complete disarmament through the Arms Control and Disarmament (ACD) policy is the only course Canadian foreign policy should chart. Others suggest that a more realistic approach be adopted that, while not discouraging ACD initiatives, provides reasonable guarantees of self-protection. This area will require much closer examination by the Canadian government. In fact, it may very well become a pivotal issue over the next two years as the North American Aerospace Defense (NORAD) agreement comes up for renewal in 2001.[15]

Multi-Purpose to Special Purpose

Given the current roles and missions set forth by the government for DND, and a modest budget within which to fund activities, the Canadian Forces will continue to experience problems unless a full and complete reexamination of the above roles is undertaken. The Canadian Forces are currently committed to generating and maintaining a multi-purpose force. It may be time to re-examine those roles and conclude that "multi-purpose" is no longer an acceptable option for Canada's armed forces. Instead, Canada should define exactly what it wishes its forces to accomplish. In other words, the only viable option may be to specialize. High operational tempos, coupled with cuts to defence budgets, personnel and capital programs and no apparent support for long-term strategy to modernize aging fleets, have eroded the military's ability to perform as an effective multi-purpose force. For nearly thirty years, Canada has undertaken to reduce force structures whilst taking on greater and greater responsibility in a multitude of well-intentioned areas. And while Canada enjoys an esteemed position with "soft power" initiatives such as ACD, our allies have become less tolerant with Canada's inability to meet its share of the "hard power" burden of collective defence. While few question Canada's commitment to ideals, many now question the value of Canada's "token" contribution.[16]

Air Force Doctrine

One of the main thrusts of this paper is to examine how Canada's air force should cope with the changes of the next twenty years. As such, we will focus the remainder of the paper on Canadian air force issues specifically. In order to establish the groundwork, the air force's first order of business should be the development of new doctrine that clearly identifies specific roles and tasks that Canada can credibly undertake. This new doctrine must be visionary and over-arching, yet relevant and clearly understood by the members of the service and, most importantly, validated by government - which funds and employs the air force. It must be flexible, yet rigid enough to clearly articulate the roles that the government wishes to be performed. It must be evolutionary and not tied to outdated Cold War strategies. Doctrine is the foundation upon which more specific guidance in forms such as the White Paper and Defence Planning Guidance can be articulated. A mechanism must be put in place to facilitate "re-visitation" by senior defence planners to ensure it remains consistent with any strategic guidance the government issues. Clearly, both the military leadership and political hierarchy must agree upon doctrine, which provides sound direction and a clear mandate on how the CF should operate over the long term. While this is not how air force policy has been historically developed, history has indeed changed and the CF and the government must adapt. In this context, doctrinal guidance provides the checks and balances necessary to ensure new roles, missions and equipment initiatives are consistent with the government's long-term policy goals for the air force.

To further the development and maintenance of doctrine for the Canadian Air Force, it is highly recommended that consideration be given to formulating an air doctrine cell at the Canadian Forces College, staffed by a small detachment from the Chief of the Air Staff organization. The co-location of the air force doctrine cell with an Armed Forces College is an approach already adopted by the USAF and the RAF. The advantage of this collaborative effort resides principally in the resources and expertise readily available to the doctrine planners. Because the Canadian Forces College represents the centre of excellence for advanced military studies in Canada, it would provide an ideal venue for an Air Force doctrine cell dedicated to studying and advancing air doctrine applicable to Canada's air force.

New Force Structures

Formal approval of the doctrine is essential before the air force can proceed with revitalizing the force structure, equipment and funding needed to perform the roles and missions outlined in the doctrine. The force structure must be credible and self-sustaining for specified lengths of time. On the first issue, manning levels and funding must be sufficient to carry out all of the newly directed roles and missions. On the second issue, savings that are realized through force re-structuring, discarded or reduced taskings, and capital equipment must be reinvested into specialty roles, missions and equipment.[17] In essence, some hard decisions will have to be made regarding fleet composition and size. Based on the roles and missions articulated by the government and outlined in the air force doctrine, a CF-18 Rapid Reaction Force (RRF(A)) concept will demand a leaner and more capable force. Funding for refurbishment programs to upgrade avionics, weapons systems and survive-to-operate (STO) contingency support may need to come from the sale of residual CF-18s not identified in the force structure. In other words, for the CF-18 fleet to survive and modernize, at least one squadron complement of the 122 CF-18s may have to be sold. While these measures may appear draconian, the intent is not to eliminate the fleet, but to bolster its capability in areas such as sovereignty patrol and rapid-reaction. Finding funds to re-equip a fully sustainable fighter force that is both potent and credible must be the ultimate goal. Additional funding initiatives are explored in further detail later in the paper.

The issue of fleet realignment will be a difficult task to manage. There will be airframes and fleets destined for foreign sale. The Aircraft Management Committee (AMC) will need to identify those fleets that do not fully exploit the capabilities for which they were intended and do not support the new specialty roles outlined in doctrine. Similarly, the role of strategic airlift will have to be carefully examined and creative initiatives to bolster this capability may have to be sought. Strategic airlift capabilities amongst all allied nations - in particular the United States - have been stretched to the limit and management of these High Value Air Assets (HVAA) to guarantee continued support is critical. Allies, including Canada, may wish to examine the possibility of a centrally managed strategic airlift capability similar to that of NATO's Airborne Early Warning (NAEW) fleet of E-3A aircraft. Whether these assets are centrally located or remain organic to the nation who owns them, fleets may be identified as NATO and/or UN contingency assets and made available when needed. Other initiatives may involve out-sourcing, contingency contracting, and military-to-military Memoranda of Understanding (MOU) in order to guarantee the air force's capability in this area.

Interoperability

Clearly, interoperability with Canada's allies must be a high priority. Information systems, weapons systems, training and operations must be compatible with those of Canada's allies. Canada must also endeavor to find ways to gain comparative advantage in technologies and roles that its allies do not fully exploit, and are essential force multipliers to any coalition force structure. Where possible, the air force should ensure that new roles and technologies support unilateral foreign policy agendas in areas such as domestic and international assistance operations in addition to those needed to support collective defence arrangements. Conversely, air force platforms and technologies that provide domestic services not available in the private sector can not be discarded because they have a limited role in other defence arrangements. Where it is feasible, every effort should be made to ensure that such platforms are capable of performing secondary roles.

Financial Solutions

Fiscal pressures have been and will continue to be a major factor in the determination of air force programs. Governments continue to seek methods of deficit management and the public, with its long list of other demands for government funding, is generally not supportive of maintaining previous defence spending levels in the aftermath of the Cold War. In addition, there are pressures internal to the department affecting air force funding. Competition between the three environments and central systems has resulted in a downward trend over the past few years regarding the CC3 (Air Force) portion of the budget. Meanwhile, the employment of air power in conflict resolution, peace support operations and on the domestic scene, has been on the increase. This paradox places particular stresses on the air force planner. Consequently, to meet the fiscal challenges ahead, the air force must take certain precautionary measures.

Recent initiatives such as OPRAM have forced severe pressure on the air force to downsize. Unfortunately, this has resulted in shortages in planning staff that the air force will need to adequately meet the challenges of the future. One of the primary assets to be considered as the air force moves forward under restrictive budgets, will be its financial planning staff. Personnel reductions in this area have been as high as 60% over the recent past. Planning staffs must be augmented with a cadre of knowledgeable, astute and proactive financial mangers who are cognizant of the tight fiscal environment prevalent today. These individuals must be aware of the financial systems, procedures and tools at their disposal, versed in the plethora of financial programs coming online, familiar with the fiscal pressures being exerted, and knowledgeable about their origins. Only then will they be capable of handling the unpredictable changes inherent in the new fiscal environment. Furthermore, this cadre of professional financial planners will need to be augmented with air force members throughout the chain of command who are aware of their financial responsibilities and learn to make sound, informed financial decisions.

It is clear that there will have to be an increase in the proportion of DND budgets allocated to capital to prevent further deterioration of CF weapons systems, aircraft and equipment. It is also clear that the air force cannot expect central systems to fund all of its needs. Consequently, CC3 funding profiles will need to be adjusted to raise some of the capital within the air force. In addition, the air force must conduct operations even more efficiently than it currently does and explore and implement creative and perhaps extraordinary ways of managing our current resources. The Contingency Review Initiative is focussing on options to address this particular issue. This work should continue. All options that are within current financial regulations, even if they are creative proposals that push the boundaries of those regulations, should be pursued. A sound business case may find favourable hearing within Treasury Board and Cabinet under the current tight fiscal environment. Some ideas are briefly explored below.

In an effort to rationalize or pare down fleets to raise capital funding, the air force should consider selling some of its aircraft, together with spare parts inventories through Foreign Military Sales programs. This new capital could be set aside until needed to fund upgrades or new capital purchases. All sorts of arrangements are possible from simple sales of aircraft and equipment to special rental agreements and shared usage programs that could generate much-needed capital.

Prospects exist whereby special partnerships with industry could prove beneficial to the air force. Some of these options have been pursued under D2000 and Alternate Service Delivery programs, such as the contracting out of complete training programs as experienced at Portage, la Prairie, Manitoba, or innovative service support arrangements such as that carried out by Serco in Goose Bay; however, there are still opportunities for further savings. These options should, nevertheless, be continually reviewed against core capabilities to ensure that they do not inadvertently erode capabilities or competencies required to sustain primary tasks. To this end, the air force could utilize the cadre of financial officers discussed above to bolster internal studies in these areas.

Increasingly, the air force is required to deploy to meet immediate operational requirements that were unforeseen in the original yearly budget estimates. While no one can ever plan well for the unexpected, it is possible to put in place financial programs and procedures to cover a host of contingencies that would alleviate the need to rob ongoing programs, thereby creating the financial crunch that accompanies most non-forecasted operations. Obviously, this is often outside the reach of the air force, but this should not preclude the precipitation of discussions that may permit lead agencies to define a new way ahead. The air force should lead the charge to seek mandated agreements that would require requisite incremental funding to be made available by the requesting authority whenever contingency operations are initiated. While this may seem somewhat naïve, the premise is built on sound ethical, procedural and financial principles which higher authorities cannot ignore. In the event that this fails, parallel efforts should be conducted to resolve the issue in-house. This could begin with a reasonable assessment of the most likely scenarios wherein Canada would be asked to provide air power and an assessment of the level of involvement. This funding requirement, identified in the normal Business Plan as a contingency requirement, would, obviously, be an unfunded requirement. Nevertheless, its new profile would lend visibility to the requirement perhaps gaining acknowledgement in the Defence Planning Guide (DPG) process. Actual funding could be provided on loan from air force Investment Accounts as discussed below.

Funds received from special sales or rental initiatives noted above should be wisely invested until required for capital or contingency use. The Department has not been proactive in this area. Revenues are returned annually to the Receiver General, but never invested or earmarked to offset upcoming programs. At the very least, interest-bearing accounts should be considered to earn some return on the funding. However, even more innovative investments could prove beneficial to the Department and the air force. Special arrangements can be negotiated through industry to participate in cost-sharing programs, research and development (with shares in royalties returning to the Investment Account), phased purchasing agreements, partnerships in maintenance, shared inventory arrangements and similar innovations. These Investment Accounts could be managed exclusively within CC3, or central systems could manage accounts on behalf of all three environments. They would provide much-needed seed money for air force programs.

Canada and the air force cannot afford to sit idly by as other nations race ahead in the information age. This behaviour would be wholly out of context with the traditional Canadian practice of "getting involved". Every effort must be made to engage Canadian industry in high-tech enterprises that demonstrate potential for capturing a share of the information pie. Other forums to exploit include the Canadian Space Agency, the CF Chief of Research and Development (CRAD), the CF Directorate of Science and Technology Air Defence and Research and Development (DSTA), the US Defense Advanced Research Projects

Agency (DARPA), USSSPACECOM, and the European Cooperation for the Long Term in Defence (EUCLID).

It is our belief that our most critical asset is our people. The most advanced technology, the best aircraft and weapons systems, the finest equipment and supporting systems and facilities will not win a war or be effective in peace support, humanitarian or domestic operations without properly trained, highly skilled and motivated individuals operating them. Certainly, some of the answers lie in strong and effective leadership, but others lie in a host of Quality-of-Life (QOL) issues that will require concerted effort and the expenditure of funds. There is a significant push within the Department, primarily as a result of the SCONDVA resolutions, to address some long-term shortcomings in this regard. Whereas these are sorely needed and welcome, the Air Force will need to address some particular areas of concern within its own sphere of influence.

It is clearly time for an air force "Personnel-First" program to implement the needed changes. Leadership aspects of this program involve changes to our training programs that would emphasize people and incorporate many of the new ideas available on motivation, work environments, work relationships, etc. It must emphasize that the air force is a disciplined organization with a mandate to perform. But, likewise, it must also show that it is a most enjoyable place to work filled with unique opportunities, exciting roles and interesting people. This Personnel-First program should carry on where SCONDVA left off, seeking out areas that are unique within the air force and within air force responsibilities requiring attention. It should be a conduit for ideas from serving members and their families to authorities as well as a pipeline from SCONDVA initiatives down to the people in uniform.

Pay, compensation and benefits (including pensions) should be attractive, exceeding similar packages outside the Department, so that good people are retained and the air force can attract quality people from the Canadian population. There is every reason to believe that the climate is right for more reasonable compensation packages to the military in light of press coverage from recent domestic assistance operations.

Conclusion

While no one can completely forecast where air power might end up twenty years from now, there are a number of steps the Canadian Air Force can effectively take to ensure that it is ready to meet the challenges that lie ahead. Clearly, doctrinal issues that spell out specific roles, missions, force structures and the equipment needed to perform special roles need to be ironed out. Threats to Canada's security and to the globe will require refocusing on domestic defence initiatives and may well draw Canada into the BMD sphere in some form. The air force will need to find new and innovative ways to pay for specialisation, but the most daunting task will be to identify those roles, missions and systems that the air force should not do and cannot afford. It will be in these areas that the air force will find the savings to invest in the new and more specialised roles. Interoperability will play a pivotal role as new information systems race ahead. In this area, Canada cannot exclude itself. Quality-of-life issues will require new initiatives to maintain high levels of morale and entice new members to the air force team. The challenge will be to accomplish all of these feats with budgets that are not expected to change dramatically and through a period where uncertainty and instability will dominate the agenda.

Notes

1. Giulio Douhet, *The Command of Air*, 1921.
2. Richard P. Hallion, "Air Power and the Changing Nature of War", *Joint Force Quarterly,* Autumn/Winter 197-1998, p. 44.
3. Department of National Defence, *Strategy Overview 1998* (Ottawa: DND Canada, 1999), p. iii.
4. "The smal and the Many: CDS Issues Seminar at the Canadian Forces College", http://www.cfc.dnd.ca/CDS_Issues/contents/Mr897_1_e.html
5. US Military Doctrine, *Joint Vision 2021: America's Military. Preparing for Tomorrow.*
6. Martin van Creveld, "The Rise and Fall of Air Power," *Military History Quarterly*, Vol. 8 (Spring 1996).
7. Stephen Biddle, "Victory Misunderstood: What the Gulf War Tells us about the Future of Conflict," *International Security*, Vol. 21, No. 2 (Fall 1996).
8. Canada, "Preparing for the Next War: Reflections on the Revolution in Military Affairs," http://www.vcds.dnd.ca/CDS_Issues/contents/MR880_3_E.html, 1998.
9. Ibid.
10. *Joint Vision 2010*, p. 1.
11. Air Force Doctrine Document, *Organization and Employment of Aerospace Power*, 28 September 1998, p. 45.
12. *Joint Vision 2010,* p. 45.
13. Canada, "An Information-Based Revolution in Military Affairs", http://www.vcds.dnd.dnd.ca/vcds/dgsp/c...t/cdsissues/contents/MR880_4_E.SAP, 1998.
14. "Defence Planning Guidance 1999, http://www.vcds.dnd.ca/vcds/dgsp/dpg/dpg99/Intro_e.asp, 1998,p. 1.
15. Ibid., p. 16.
16. Clark Campbell, "Spend More Money on Defence, US Envoy Tells Canada," http://www.nationalpost.com/home.asp?f=990112/21742611, 12 January 1999.
17. Richard Szanfranski, "Annulling Marriages: Reframing the Roles, Missions, and Functions Debate," *Airpower Journal*, Winter 1993, p. 55-67.

Air Power Theory

Lieutenant-Colonel Sylvain Lepage, Major Pierre Carignan, Major John Foster, Major Ken Groen, Major Les Jones, Major Daniel Pilon, and Lieutenant-Colonel Neville Russell

Introduction

Since the end of the Cold War the Canadian Forces have undergone major restructuring as vague military threats and calls for "peace dividends" have led to significantly smaller funding and force levels. Reduced funding has been difficult for the air force where, despite managing the majority of the Defence Services Programme, the need to procure increasingly more expensive weapons systems in order to conduct modern air operations has had an impact on day-to-day activities. These budget reductions have also been implemented in spite of the demonstrated effectiveness of air power during the Gulf War, and the success of the Bosnian peace negotiations where air power ultimately encouraged the Serbs to sign the Dayton Accords.

What then makes the "selling" of air power so difficult? Carl Builder, a leading American air power commentator, has suggested that the United States Air Force (USAF) has recently suffered huge budget cuts, relative to its sister services, because of a lack of air power theory to support the USAF's existence as a separate service. His appeal to use air power theory, as a means of shaping defence policy, is based on his claim that it would provide a more rational criterion for developing defence policy than those factors currently used.[1]

In this paper, we will illustrate the importance of an air power theory to develop a coherent and focused mission, vision, and doctrine for Canada's air force. Further, in order to stimulate discussion, we will propose a universal air power theory and, based on this theory, we will develop and propose a new mission and a new vision for the Canadian Air Force.

To start, we will define air power and its inherent characteristics. Secondly, we will define and establish the relationship of four related but different conceptual terms - theory, mission, vision, and doctrine - and discuss the impact of the absence of a theory on the other three elements. Thirdly, we will demonstrate the relevance of an air power theory and its importance to Canada. Finally, we will offer our proposals for a theory, a mission, and a vision for the Canadian Air Force.

Defining Air Power[2]

> In a world where access to other points on the surface may be increasingly jeopardized by intervening regions of disorder or hostility, the third dimension may be the most confident, secure, and rapid means for access. In a world of widespread political disorder and conflict, the third dimension may also be the most confident and secure vantage point for observing and then discriminatingly applying military power. Thus, even as the relative powers of the nation-states decline, there is more rather than less to suggest that air power has become the military instrument of choice for coping with the new disorder of a world undergoing revolutionary change.[3]
>
> Carl Builder

Air power, due to its inherent characteristics and differences from the other elements, is the predominant instrument of military forces that can utilize, exploit, and maximize the use of the third dimension to win wars. However, for the purposes of this essay, we will limit our discussion of air power to its employment within the atmosphere.

The characteristics of the air environment offer perspective (in terms of elevation) and freedom of movement (three-dimensional manoeuvre), which simply cannot be achieved in the land and sea environments. This perspective and freedom of movement can, in turn, provide a freedom of action and universal access that is unparalleled when compared to the land and sea environments. The ability to deploy military power over long distances at high speeds offers great advantages that can only be provided by air power.

The air medium allows commanders to disperse, concentrate, and manoeuvre air forces to obtain universal observation of the earth's surface. Also, the air medium exposes an enemy's entire power structure to assault by air forces. Control of the surface battle in modern conventional warfare is dependent upon control of the air over friendly and enemy territory.

Air power is fundamentally different from land or sea power due to the environment in which it operates, and because of the platforms that have been developed to exploit the environment. Air power can be applied sequentially or simultaneously through independent, integrated (joint and/or combined), and supporting or supported operations conducted at all levels of war at the same time.

Characteristics of Air Power[4]

The technological exploitation of the properties and characteristics of the air environment permit the production of platforms that have greater speed, range, elevation, manoeuvrability, and freedom of action than platforms produced to operate in the land and sea environments. As a result, air power has the following inherent characteristics:

    a.   <u>Responsiveness</u>. A virtually unimpeded (except for very adverse weather) freedom of movement allows greater mobility. Greater mobility, when combined with greater speed, permits greater responsiveness. It can be used to counter, or pose simultaneous threats across a far wider geographical area than is possible with land surface or sea systems. Air power can be deployed rapidly into distant theatres to provide visible and timely support to an ally, or act as a deterrent to aggression without forward-basing, or deploying standing forces. Essentially, the responsiveness of air power provides flexibility in strategic planning by enabling the commander to react swiftly, effectively, and decisively in any given situation;

    b.   <u>Flexibility</u>. Aircraft can perform a wide variety of tasks, produce a wide range of effects, and be adapted with comparative ease to meet changing circumstances and situations. Given their freedom of movement, range, elevation, and speed, aircraft can be diverted to new tasks while airborne, or reconfigured for new tasks while on the ground;

    c.   <u>Versatility</u>. Air power can be employed equally effectively at the strategic, operational, and tactical levels of warfare. Air power's versatility offers choice regarding the duration, scale and continuity of commitment; the variety, distribution and location of targets; variations in intensity and weight of attack. Platforms such as fighters can be configured for air-to-air and air-to-surface missions simultaneously. They can also fulfil a variety of offensive and defensive roles. Air power can be used simultaneously and continuously against a broad spectrum of targets, and with sufficient force to overwhelm the enemy;

d. Stealth. The size and speed of air vehicles, coupled with their ability to move freely in three dimensions, makes detection and forewarning of air attack inherently difficult. Stealth is a continually developing technology that was demonstrated very successfully in the Gulf War. The incorporation of this technology on air platforms aids in their survivability by reducing their ability to be detected by radar;

e. Concentration. Speed, range, and flexibility allow air power to concentrate military force in time and space, when and where required. The ability to deliver massive destructive power at long range and with little warning is of cardinal importance in war;

f. Precision. Precision is becoming a fundamental element of air power as a result of significantly better accuracy in navigation, targeting systems, and weapons. Precision has given commanders the ability to attack the enemy with great accuracy while minimizing collateral damage and civilian casualties. In addition, precision and the characteristics of speed, range, and stealth give air power a unique ability to strike at the heart of the enemy, without having to set foot on enemy ground;

g. Elevation. Increased elevation provides a broader and deeper field of view. The ability to operate over a variety of heights gives air power the ability to observe and dominate activities on the surface and below the sea;

h. Rapidity. Using the third dimension, air power can deploy anywhere in the world, within hours, to deter attack, to prevent a crisis from escalating, or to halt a conflict;

i. <u>Lethality</u>. With factors such as speed, range, precision, concentration, and stealth, concentrated fire can be directed at specific points on and behind the battle area, and provide massed combat power. Its ability to strike effectively, quickly, and decisively with the right type of munitions at the right place and time makes air power a very lethal force.

Some of the above characteristics are shared to varying degrees with land and sea power, but it is their synergism, which is generated only in the third dimension, that makes air power indispensable to military forces called upon to project power and win wars. Carl Builder summarizes the importance of air power thus:

> Because that is the way to avoid your worst nightmare of stalemated, bloody war. To strike at the heart of the enemy without fighting your way across the ground, without inviting the nightmare, you have to strike through the third dimension, and that means air power.[5]

Air power does have some limitations like impermanence, vulnerability, unit cost, weather, etc., but these limitations are not unique to air power. No vehicle can operate indefinitely without logistical support, nor is any vehicle invulnerable. Unit cost is relative when one considers the cost of a ship and its limitations. Weather will affect any military operation. While these limitations must be considered when air power is applied, they are not relevant to the air power theory discussion and the purpose of this essay.

Theory, Mission, Vision, and Doctrine – Definitions

In discussing air power theory, four conceptual terms - theory, mission, vision and doctrine - will be used frequently. In order to ensure a common starting point, it is worthwhile to briefly discuss these four terms, and the synergy that exists between them.

Theory is defined by the Concise Oxford Dictionary as a "... supposition or system of ideas explaining something, especially one based on general principles independent of the facts, phenomena, etc., to be explained."[6] Carl Builder, in his book *The Icarus Syndrome*, states, "A theory is a supposition or conjecture about the relationships between things. Theories explain *why*."[7] Harold Winton's definition is somewhat more rigid; he adds the requirements that a theory must be in writing and systematic, "... one may define a theory as a codified, systematic body of propositions related to a particular phenomenon or field of study."[8] Central to each of these definitions is the notion that a theory is an idea or proposition describing how and why things work. Therefore, for the purposes of this paper, a theory is defined as a supposition or idea explaining how and why things work or should work.

The Oxford Concise Dictionary defines vision as an "... imaginative insight; statesmanlike foresight, sagacity in planning."[9] Builder expands on this definition, "A vision is an imagined objective, a conception of what can and ought to be. Visions provide a coherent basis for future decisions... An institutional vision is a conception of what the organization can and ought to be and be about."[10] In this paper we have adopted Builder's definition verbatim.

The Oxford Dictionary and Carl Builder largely agree on the definition of a mission. The dictionary defines mission as a "task to be performed; military operation, especially the dispatch of aircraft or spacecraft."[11] Builder describes a mission as "a task or function that is assigned or adopted" adding that, "Missions declare purpose."[12] Once again, Builder's definition has been adopted for use in this paper.

Finally, doctrine is defined in the Oxford Concise Dictionary as, "what is taught, body of instruction; religious, political, scientific, etc., belief, dogma, or tenet."[13] *Out of the Sun: Aerospace Doctrine for the Canadian Forces* describes doctrine as:

> Comprised of principles, theories and policies, accepted as valid and reliable, which offer military forces good chances for success when applied in periods of tension, crisis or war ... Doctrine is, in essence, "that which is taught." It is an accumulation of knowledge, which is gained primarily from the study and analysis of experience. As such, doctrine reflects what works best.[14]

In this paper, doctrine is defined as a set of principles based on knowledge and experience that can be taught and that outline the best means to achieve objectives.

Theory, Mission, Vision, and Doctrine - Relationship

More difficult than defining the terms is describing their relationships and synergy with each other. All four concepts are inter-related and inter-dependent to a certain degree. Which comes first? Must a theory be developed before a vision can be constructed and a mission assigned?

Does our assigned mission determine our vision, or does our vision determine what our mission will be?

These are not simple questions to answer. However, based on the definitions offered above, the following hierarchy has been developed for this paper. In a chronological sense the theory comes first. Developing a workable theory for how air power should be employed is the first step in determining the mission and building a vision. Although it may be possible to develop vision, mission, and doctrine in the absence of a theory, it will certainly be more difficult and less likely to stand the rigours of time. Certainly, without the central focus provided by air power theory, it is likely that the mission, vision, and doctrine will be suboptimal. It can be said then, that the theory provides the focus or the guiding principle for the development of the mission and vision. As Builder states:

> Theory would seem to be the most fundamental; it supposes how things will or should work...and why we should care. Given a theory of how things might work, it is a much shorter intellectual step to suggest tasks that should be taken up (a mission), to conceive what can and ought to be (a vision), and to plan the relationships between means and ends (a strategy).[15]

Second in the hierarchy is the mission. It is the mission that determines the purpose. Knowing what must be done precedes having a vision of how it should be done, and logically follows the development of a theory which proposes that it can be done. In considering the mission, however, care must be exercised to ensure that the focus on the current mission does not limit the vision of the future and of future missions. For this reason, the relationship between mission and vision is very close. This relationship is cyclical to some extent; initially, the vision is based on the current mission, but once the vision is developed it may, in turn, cause the mission to be re-assessed.

A vision of how the mission can and ought to be executed may be developed once a theory has been established and a mission stemming from the theory adopted. Vision will provide a goal for planners on which they may base future decisions. For example, the vision of how the Canadian Forces may best accomplish its sovereignty defence mission will influence what types of air assets are procured. This is where the close relationship between mission and vision can be seen. If asset selection is based on the vision, and the asset chosen offers new capabilities, in addition to those required by the current mission, the mission itself may be modified to capitalize on this additional capability. In other words, even though the vision is essentially a prediction of how the current mission may best be accomplished, the mission itself is not "fixed" and cannot be so rigid that it does not capitalize on opportunities afforded by the vision.

Doctrine differs from the other three conceptual terms by virtue of its more universal, generic nature. It permeates all three of the other concepts. Because doctrine is the product of experience and knowledge, it incorporates a variety of influences. These include old theories (or the lack thereof), societal pressures, political pressures, past successes and failures, and technological advances, all of which leave an indelible mark on existing doctrine. In a sense, it forms a slowly evolving yet constant backdrop to the development of theory, mission, and vision. Dr Richard Hallion, discussing the relationship between technology and doctrine, states:

> Both technology and doctrine are dynamic processes, always advancing or receding, and are necessarily adaptive to change lest they stagnate and lose relevance. Neither is independent of the other; rather each generates a synergistic impulse that encourages and strengthens the other.[16]

This statement is equally true of the relationship between doctrine and theory, mission, and vision. Consequently, theory finds its genesis in the extant doctrine. Theory, once developed, can cause the doctrine to evolve. Thus a theory can find its roots in doctrine and doctrine may be the product of a theory. Similarly, doctrine may be useful in developing both the mission and vision, but has its roots in lessons learned from past missions and visions. It can be said, therefore, that theory is both a resource for the development of the other three, and a product of them.

Figure 1 on the following page graphically summarizes and represents the relationship between theory, mission, vision, and doctrine, and their relations with the environment.

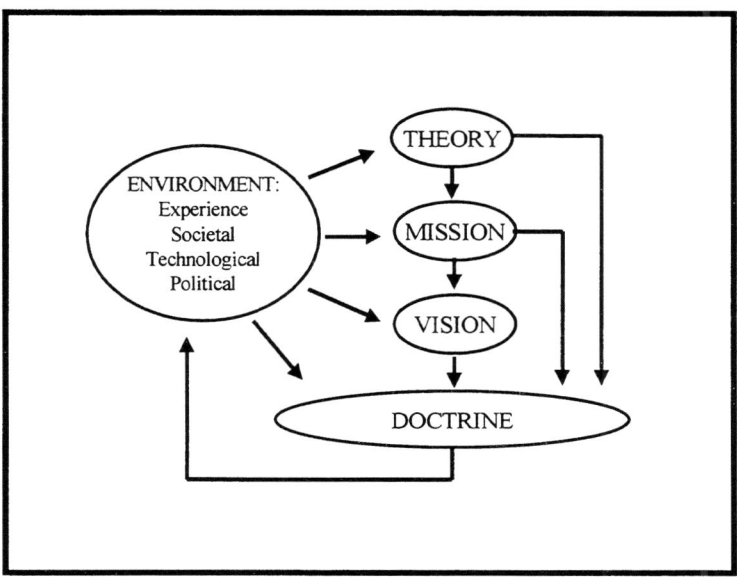

Figure 1—Hierarchy

Theory, Mission, Vision, and Doctrine - Synergy

As illustrated in Figure 1, a hierarchy is proposed; however, it is difficult to picture the synergy among the theory, mission, vision, and doctrine of air power. By using an analogy, the following paragraphs will illustrate the synergy air power gains from well-thought-out and mutually-supporting theory, mission, vision, and doctrine. Picture the air power concept as a sphere, such as an atom within its environment as illustrated in Figure 2. An atom consists of a nucleus and a number of surrounding electrons that makes the atom unique, almost indivisible and homogeneous. Similarly, air power consists of air power theory (the nucleus) and supporting mission, vision, and doctrine (the electrons). The environment is made from human actions such as experiences, new technologies, cultural changes, and political considerations. Without the synergies that arise when all four elements are in play in the environment, air power may be sub-optimized.

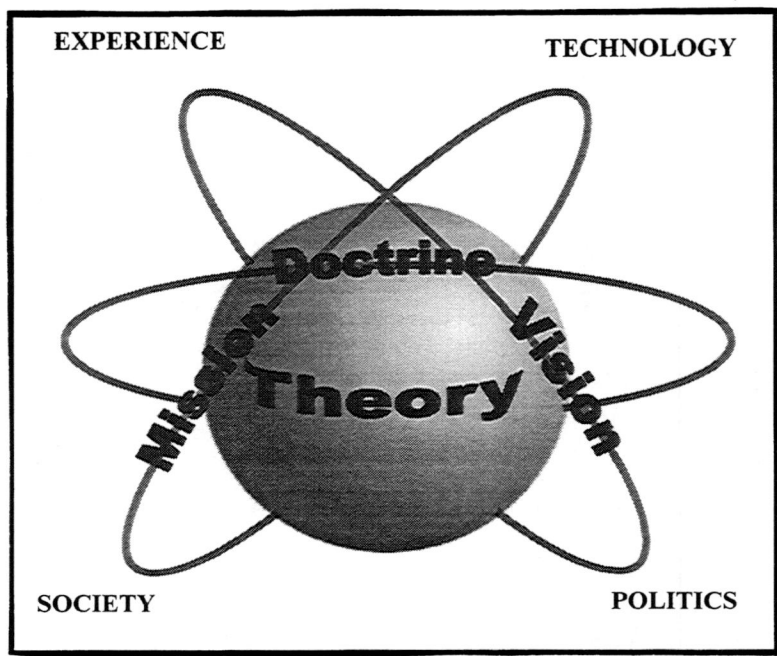

Figure 2 – The Air Power Sphere

Each element contributes to the effectiveness of the other elements and the overall ability of an air force to project air power. As previously mentioned, in order to provide focus, an air force mission and vision must be developed from an air power theory.[17] Developing the mission based on the theory will ensure that the mission will not become side-tracked, and that it will be developed from a unique source. Air power starts to gain its homogeneous property. Air power can possibly exist with only current missions to perform and a doctrine to drive forces; however, the concept will be flawed if unforeseen tasks or missions are assigned. With a proper vision, missions can be adjusted for future decisions. This ability to perceive new ideas is essential to project air power, as it will rectify any flaws found in the current mission. With the relationship between mission and vision being very close, air power starts to gain an indivisible property.

Further, as Clausewitz noted, theory yields the fundamental truths that serve as a foundation for doctrine.[18] Moreover, according to the Royal Air Force and the Australian Defence Forces, a theory - the outcome of strategic thought - contributes to the development of a doctrine.[19] Even more dramatically, Volume 3 of *the Canadian Military Aerospace Power* states that when doctrine is ignored, the result is often disastrous.[20] Without the crucial element that is doctrine, the air power concept would suffer greatly. Doctrine makes air power unique and robust.

The synergy generated from an environment, a nucleus, and three interrelated elements produces a unique, almost indivisible and homogeneous air power concept. If one removes one element – mission, vision or doctrine – air power still exists but loses some of its robustness and identity. If one removes its nucleus – the theory – the air power concept will not exist.

Why Do We Need an Air Power Theory?

Is air power theory crucial to a sound and effective air doctrine, and, can the elements of this air power theory be universal? Before these questions can be answered definitively, the relevance of air power theory to air power must be determined.

As stated earlier, air power is defined as the ability to exploit and capitalize on the third dimension. However, the ability of nations to accomplish this constantly changes as new weapon systems and aircraft technologies arise. Likewise, air power theorists must adapt to these changes and endeavour to continually interpret the impact of new land, sea, and air threats on the inherent characteristics of air power. Although most theorists have been able to explain what air power can do, few have succeeded in demonstrating that an air power theory can represent the glue which binds an air force together and influencing its direction.[21] In his article *Reflections on the Search for Air Power Theory*, I. Bholley states:

> Much of what has been written on the subject is not, strictly speaking, air power theory at all but descriptions of varied efforts to implement the conception of such theory.[22]

Theory is not a direct guide to action, but rather it educates the mind so that some useful order can be imposed to influence or direct the way air power should be employed. According to von Clausewitz:

> Theory cannot equip the mind with formulas for solving problems, nor can it mark the narrow path on which the sole solution is supposed to lie by planting a hedge of principles on either side. But it can give the mind insight into the great mass of phenomena and of their relationships, then leave it free to rise into the higher realms of action.[23]

It is through an understanding of these relationships that the overall requirement for an air power theory is born. By providing insight into the relationship between power projection and air power, air power theory can define the utility of an air force beyond its simple support to the army and navy. Without power projection, the air force would simply become a supporting arm and an extension to the navy or army. The air power of an air force is an element of national power, and often the only means to directly and decisively attack an enemy's strategic centre of gravity. Furthermore, once a nation is fully engaged in war, a successful air campaign can dramatically reduce friendly casualties, thereby protecting what is often its own centre of gravity – its national will. Last but not least, its speed, portability, fast reaction, and ability to concentrate firepower make it the preferred choice to deter acts of aggression.

Harold Winton claims that a comprehensive theory of air power does not exist.[24] If this statement is true, and one supports the idea that doctrine and theory are inextricably woven and self-supporting, current air doctrine in the US, UK, and Canada may be proven to be deficient without the development of a national or global air power theory. Thus a country that lacks an air power theory will have difficulty in projecting air power. Further, its air force will have weak guidance for the conduct of its missions, for the acquisition of its equipment, and for the training of its personnel.

Even if current air doctrines are valid, air power theory can only complement the legitimacy of an air force. A sound theory can provide justification for doctrinal changes, and ensure that the necessary tools are available to react to future technology advances in the aerospace medium, and the changing world environment. In summary, the concept of an air power theory is crucial to any modern air force. It provides focus on what matters to an air-fighting force, and can easily justify its existence. As Builder stated, "the air force mission and vision must stand on a theory of air power – an explanation of how air power works and why it is important to those who support it."[25]

The History and the Importance of Air Power Theory to Canada

The history of the application of air power in Canada provides excellent examples of both the importance of air power theory and the problems that occur if a country does not have one. Canada has never had a formal, written air power theory, but it has applied the principles of air power on occasion. During war the requirements of air power are self-evident, and Canada's success in its application during the two World Wars and during much of the early Cold War proves this point. As the following paragraphs will illustrate, the real problems for the Canadian Air Force have occurred during the inter-war periods when it searched for missions without reference to air power theory.

The employment of air power by Canada can be traced to the provision of aircrews and aircraft to the Royal Flying Corps (RFC) during the First World War. By the end of the war, fully one quarter of RFC aircrew were Canadian. This gave the nation a cadre of individuals who experienced the first large-scale military applications of the airplane. However, following the war, and in the absence of air power theory, the Royal Canadian Air Force (RCAF) was relegated to missions such as aerial surveillance. While these missions were important to the country, they had nothing to do with the application of air power. There was no Canadian equivalent to Billy Mitchell in the RCAF.

As the world approached war again during the late 1930s, Canada decided to reinvest in the RCAF. At the start of the war it had eight squadrons including fighter, army co-operation, bomber, flying boat, and torpedo bomber.[26] During the war, the RCAF offered a balanced application of air power and achieved great success in the areas of strategic bombing, offensive and defensive counter-air, counter-surface including anti-submarine warfare, and air transport. Almost 250,000 Canadians served with the RCAF in this period, and it became the fourth largest air force of the Allied Powers.[27] The success of the RCAF during the Second World War was due largely to the understanding and application of the principles of air power theory.

Immediately following the war, the Minister of National Defence for Air, Colonel The Hon. Colin Gibson, outlined the future for the RCAF. It would continue to be a balanced force of about 16,000 regular personnel and eight operational squadrons including two bomber reconnaissance squadrons, two transport squadrons, one fighter reconnaissance squadron, and one fighter-bomber squadron.[28] The Minister understood the application of air power, in both offensive and defensive applications, and attempted to structure the RCAF along those lines. Unfortunately, this direction was not supported by the government, which failed to see a threat to the western world. The RCAF was reduced to a force of 11,000. Air Defence Group and 410 Fighter Squadron were equipped with the Vampire fighter aircraft which was ineffective and incapable of projecting power. The RCAF, one of the world's largest airforces only five years earlier, "was not in a position to send a fighter squadron to Korea in support of the UN. A lack of trained personnel after demobilization coupled with a significant period of time required to re-establish a fighter organization in Canada were contributing factors."[29]

The Korean War led to the Cold War, and for the first time in modern history Canada faced the possibility of a direct attack on its soil. Canadian defence spending tripled between 1950 and 1953[30] sparked by a renewed interest in air power which marked the heyday for the RCAF:

> The February 1951 budget contained a five billion dollar expenditure over three years, of which almost half was for the re-equipping of the RCAF.... The RCAF would equal the army in total number of personnel... (e)arlier on 1 Aug 1950, Air Defence Group had assumed the responsibility for anti-aircraft defence by incorporating the headquarters of Army Anti-Aircraft Command into its organization.[31]

Canadian air power was also exercised in other areas. Maritime Air Group was formed in 1953, and 1 Canadian Air Division was established in Europe with four fighter wings, each with 12 squadrons (nine of F-86 Sabres and three CF-100 Canucks). In Canada, Air Defence Command operated 162 CF-100 interceptors by 1955. For the first time since the Second World War, and the last time in its history, the RCAF was capable of projecting power.

The year 1959 saw the introduction of the first White Papers outlining Canadian government priorities for National Defence. The 1959 White Paper, although very supportive of the roles of the military, initiated the transition from using a military power model to a mission-centric model to provide guidance. In other words, the government started to define missions based on equipment available rather than on air power theory. This abandonment of the principles of air power in search of specific missions began almost immediately. This first became evident in Europe when the Sabre was replaced with the Canadian-built CF-104 Starfighter. The RCAF favoured the McDonnell-Douglas F-4 because of its flexibility and combat capability, but there were no industrial spin-offs to be had.[32] The government equipped the RCAF with an aircraft designed to intercept long-range bombers, and placed it in Europe to replace an air-superiority fighter. This divergence from air power theory forced the government to find a new role for the CF-104 - tactical nuclear strike. Rather than focusing on air power, the government focused on industrial benefits and subsequently lost the essential capability of air superiority.

Another significant departure from air power theory came in 1963 with the signing of the Defence Development Sharing Agreement (DDSA) which was designed to involve the Canadian defence industry in the development of selected defence items. "This agreement established the framework by which Canadian industry could be involved in the development of items required by the U.S. military."³³ This led directly to the acquisition of 100 Northrop CF-5 fighters in 1966, built by Canadair, to give the RCAF the ability to support the army. The RCAF again favoured the F-4 because of its superior combat capability and range, while the CF-5 was near the bottom of its preference list.³⁴ However, to support Canadair, the decision was made to acquire the CF-5. Initially the air force had a hard time finding a role for the aircraft. It was sent to the RCAF base in Baden to determine its usefulness in the NATO environment and eventually a new role was created for the air protection of the Alliance's northern flank (in northern Norway). Had the principles of air power been applied, the CF-5 would not have been bought. Instead, the mission-centric model had to be used to find a role for the aircraft.

What little focus on air power that remained in Canada evaporated with the disbanding of the RCAF, and the loss of the environmental headquarters in favour of the centralized NDHQ concept during unification. The air element now consisted of seven operational level headquarters and it was given responsibility for all aviation assets in the country, including tactical aviation (helicopters, tactical transports, and support fighters) and maritime rotary aviation. This massive increase in responsibility combined with the fragmentation of air force leadership (due to the multitude of independent formations) resulting in a loss of focus for the air element. At the same time, spending on new equipment dropped to less than 10 percent of the defence budget.³⁵ Air Command was formed in 1975 to regroup the air force and provide centralized direction; however, none of the ideals of air power remained and there was no vision, focus, or doctrine.

It was not until the early 1990s that command issues in the Air Force became clearer and the requirement for air force doctrine was recognized. The Commander of Air Command, LGen David Huddleston, summarized the problems encountered by the air force:

> It is easy for air forces to become fragmented in thought, given their propensity to self-identify by functional activity. We Canadians have encouraged this, however, with the study of scenario-based commitments of elements of air power. The most obvious example is that of our fighter commitments to NATO and NORAD. These have seen us focus, at various points in time, on clear air mass air combat, on all-weather intercept, on nuclear strike, on tactical reconnaissance, and on the gamut of conventional attack roles.... Even with the introduction of a single aircraft type, the CF-18, we continue to wrestle with those who would advocate their favourite role rather than promote the

strength which airpower derives from its flexibility.[36]

LGen Huddleston also suggested the way ahead, declaring "First, we must re-establish the primacy of the doctrine of the whole air force. ..."[37] However, without a firm understanding of air power theory, the doctrine lacked focus. The lack of an air power theory also impacted on the mission and vision statements released by Air Command and the Chief of the Air Staff (CAS) over the years. For example, the vision statement from the Commander of Air Command in 1996 and repeated in the 1998 Planning Guidance was:

> The air force will continue to evolve towards a sound total force team to accomplish our mission professionally, emphasising strong leadership, an optimal mix of operational capabilities, effective command and control structures, and managerial excellence.[38]

This vision, although politically correct, is uninspiring and unrelated to an air force. In fact, General Motors or Bombardier could have easily replaced the term "air force".

It is refreshing to see that this has been corrected with the release of the CAS Guidance for 1999, and the Canadian Air Force now has a vision statement, "The Canadian Air Force: Proud, Professional and Combat Capable", consistent with the principles of air power.

Throughout its history the Canadian air force in general and the RCAF in particular were at their strongest when they pursued a balanced air power theory. They were best able to serve the country and contribute to the military element of national power. The focus on air power is most easily done when the enemy is obvious. Without the guidance of air power theory it is difficult, if not impossible, particularly in times of peace, to develop enduring and practical vision, mission, and doctrinal statements. These elements, in turn, are essential to providing clear strategic direction for the air force. In the absence of air power theory, the air force will lack the cohesion and focus necessary to make the right choices for the new millennium.

Air Power Theory

For the foreseeable future, humankind will be engaged in conflict. Conflicts will arise as different nation-states or non-state actors attempt to exert their will upon others. At times, conflict will become violent and military force will be required in order to resolve it. Violent conflict may or may not result in formally declared wars.[39]

Although humankind primarily lives, works, and plays on the surface of the earth, violent conflict can occur in the land, sea, air, space, or cyberspace[40] environments. Therefore, the battlespace can encompass any or all of these environments. Theoretically, victory in violent conflict can be achieved without dominating all of the battlespace. However, without complete domination of the battlespace, or at least parity with one's adversary throughout the battlespace, the cost of victory is likely to be prohibitive. Only with complete domination of the battlespace can one guarantee victory over one's adversary and only through domination of the air environment can one guaranty freedom of action on the surface of the earth.[41]

This does not imply that surface forces cannot obtain freedom of action without air forces. It merely implies that to ensure freedom of action on the surface of the earth, domination of the air environment is essential. It is for this reason that the maritime definition for "sea control" requires control not just on and below the surface of the water, but the airspace above the water as well.[42]

The military means of dominating the battlespace will be achieved by a state's military forces applying their combat power (lethal and non-lethal). The dominant combat power exerted in the air environment will be air power. As well as dominating the air environment, air power can asymmetrically assist in striking an adversary's centre of gravity (CofG) by delivering the decisive blow, or countering the enemy's decisive blow, when and where required, using precision attacks of predominantly lethal, destructive force. Air power is capable of domination in this fashion because of its universal, rapid access, and unique vantage point.[43]

In summary, the air power theory we are about to propose is based upon the following key assumptions:

    a.   Although the Cold War has ceased, violent conflict and warfare have not. States must be prepared to engage in violent conflict and/or war in order to ensure their vital interests are safeguarded, and;

    b.   Since the Second World War, the battlespace has evolved from the land, sea, and air environments to include space and cyber-space. Lethal and non-lethal combat power can be exerted in each of these environments. Correspondingly, the sum of a nation's combat power can be considered to be land power, sea power, air power, space power, and cyber-space power. Combat power throughout these environments is necessary to guarantee victory.

Proposed Air Power Theory Statement

As long as humankind attempts to resolve conflict through violence, sovereign states will maintain air power as part of their organic combat power in order to dominate or prevent domination of the air environment. Also, air power can conduct strategic attacks by directly striking an adversary's CofG. Domination of the air environment is essential not only to enable air power to conduct a strategic attack, but also to guarantee freedom of action on the surface of the earth. The most effective means of applying air power is through centrally-controlled air forces.

Finally, because of air power's ability to strike directly at an adversary's CofG, the application of air power is no longer limited to supporting surface campaigns. Since manoeuvre warfare is centered on attacking an adversary's CofG, air power can, in its own right, become a supported element in warfare with the other elements of combat power (land, sea, space and cyberspace) becoming supporting elements.[44] Therefore, depending on the conflict, the air campaign can become the primary campaign, with the land and sea campaigns in support. This does not imply that air power can win wars independently of other forces. The battlespace is too complex for any one form of combat power to "win" independently. Air power is essential; however, it is not all-encompassing.

Why This Air Power Theory?

This theory is exclusive by design. It centers air power on combat forces designed for dominating the air environment first (counter-air operations), and then striking at an adversary's CofG second (strategic offensive operations). This is the essence of air power and, based on historical precedents, the reason for having centrally-controlled air forces.[45] It is through the experiences gained and the technological advances achieved by conducting these two types of operations that air forces, by executing successful counter-surface operations and supporting air operations, have become essential ingredients in surface campaigns.

Similarly, just as the combat power designed for dominating the air environment is air power, combat power designed for dominating the surface environments is part of that surface's combat power (similar arguments can be made for space and cyber-space power). The conclusion to be drawn from this exclusionary theory is that not all assets that use the third dimension are part of air power, just as not all assets that are on the surface of the earth are part of that surface's combat power. Those flying assets that are primarily supporting surface campaigns should be considered part of that surface's combat power. It follows then that tactical aviation assets (which are designed to dominate the land environment) should be considered part of land power. Maritime patrol assets (which are designed to dominate the sea environment) should be considered part of sea power and surface-to-air missiles (which are designed to dominate the air environment) should be considered part of air power. Therefore, to gain maximum operational effectiveness, tactical aviation assets should be grouped within the army, maritime patrol aircraft should be grouped within the navy and finally, surface-to-air missiles should be grouped within the air force. Although it will be more operationally effective to group assets in this fashion, one must recognize that it will be administratively more expensive. As such, because Canada faces no direct threat, consecutive Canadian governments have chosen to maximize administrative efficiencies over operational effectiveness by grouping all flying assets within Canada's air force.[46]

This theory is not meant to imply that elements not involved in either counter-air or strategic offensive operations should not be part of a centrally-controlled air force. Clearly, assets assigned to supporting air operations and sustainment operations are essential for successful counter-air and strategic offensive operations. Therefore, aside from the administrative synergies gained through centralization, grouping supporting air and sustainment assets under a single air force commander increases operational effectiveness.

Proposed Air Force Mission Statement

The present air force Mission Statement is:

The mission of Canada's air force is to generate and maintain combat capable, multi-purpose air forces to meet Canada's defence objectives.[47]

The present Mission Statement is valid as long as the term "multi-purpose" is restricted. Given the proposed air power theory, independent air forces exist to either dominate the air environment or asymmetrically assist in the domination of land, sea and space environments through the application of lethal, destructive force. However, there is no indication that the "multi-purpose" air forces indicated in the present Mission Statement pertain to dominating the air environment or assisting in the domination of the other environments through destructive force. Rather, "multi-purpose" is all-encompassing and means "anything that flies"[48]. Regardless of the value provided by flying assets that are not involved in "pure" air power missions, flying assets that neither directly nor indirectly contribute to these missions should not be included in the Mission Statement; or, as a minimum, it should be made clear that they are secondary in importance. Including all flying assets in the Mission Statement without clarification results in confusion as to the true mission of air forces.

The following is the proposed Mission Statement and its rationale:

The mission of Canada's air force is to generate and apply air power to meet Canada's defence objectives.

The proposed Mission Statement is preferred over the present Mission Statement because it ties the air force mission to air power theory. Although it would be ideal that all members of the air force know the definition of air power, this is unlikely to occur. Regardless, air force personnel know intuitively that air power relates to dominating the air environment. Therefore, the proposed mission statement reinforces the intuitive understanding of air power, relates the mission to the theory, and thus reinforces the rationale for centrally controlled air forces. With respect to ensuring that the CAS is aware of his responsibilities for generating assets not involved in air power, the CAS Business Plan need only identify these as assigned tasks.

Proposed Air Force Vision Statement

The present air force Vision Statement is:

The Canadian air force: Proud, Professional and Combat Capable.[49]

The present Vision Statement is satisfactory given the present Mission Statement. It conforms to the theory presented in that it flows from the Mission Statement by referring to a "combat capable" air force. As well, it provides a conception of what the organization can and ought to be and be about: proud and professional. However, this Vision Statement lacks clarity for the air force in being prepared to fight and win wars. Fighting and winning wars is why armed forces, including air forces, exist for a nation and thus should be part of what an air force ought to be and be about.

The following is the proposed Vision Statement and its rationale:

Canada's air force: ready for war, trained to win, at home and abroad, alone or in concert with our Allies.

As with the present Vision Statement, the proposed Vision Statement conforms to the theory in that flows from the proposed Mission Statement by referring to an air force "ready for war", which is why air power exists. As well, it also provides a conception of what the organization can and ought to be about: "trained to win at home and abroad, alone or in concert with our Allies". It is considered an improvement for the following reasons:

 a. Adding the term "ready for war, trained to win" makes it emphatically clear to all air force personnel that their ultimate duty is to be prepared to fight and WIN in war. In this the era of "soft power" and "peacekeeping", it becomes easier for military personnel to forget that this is why they exist. Adding this term will ensure that they do not. It is also hoped that by adding this term, procurement will be focused on those systems that directly aid in war-fighting;

 b. Adding the term "at home and abroad" makes it clear to air force personnel that they may have to apply air power in far-off places. Thus, air force personnel must have their affairs in order to ensure they are capable of deploying if/when required;

 c. Adding the term "alone" makes it clear that the air force must be self-reliant. Although it is difficult to perceive situations where Canada would "go it alone", ultimately the armed forces must be prepared to carry out their government's will independent of other nations, and;

 d. Adding the term "in concert with our allies" ensures that the air force keeps interoperability clearly in sight. In almost all cases, Canada will be involved in coalition operations, thus it is imperative that our armed forces be capable of operating with our allies, especially NATO forces. Therefore, regardless of the requirement to be capable of "going it alone", the air force must not do so to the detriment of interoperability.

Conclusion

Air power theory is crucial to any modern air force. It explains how and why air power works or should work. It provides focus for an air force's mission, vision, and doctrine, and can easily justify its existence. An air force which lacks an air power theory will not be able to provide strong guidance for the conduct of its missions, for the acquisition of its equipment, or for the training of its personnel. As a result, it will have difficulty in developing capabilities needed to project air power. Without power projection, the air force would simply become a supporting arm or an extension of the navy or army. Air power could not then be developed to its greatest potential and the government would not be able to realize the maximum benefits from of a key element of national power.

Canada has never had a formally accepted air power theory, but throughout its history the Canadian Air Force was at its strongest when it applied the principles of a balanced air power theory. The problems for the Canadian Air Force have occurred during the inter-war periods and since the early 1960s when successive governments chose to give guidance based on mission-centric models rather than on air power theory. As a result the air force has floundered, searching for a mission in order to sell itself, instead of using air power theory to solidify the air force's *raison d'être*, influence defence policy, and provide the government with the power projection capabilities it needs to support its foreign policy objectives.

This paper offers an air power theory. The theory is centered on combat forces designed for dominating the air environment first, and then striking at an adversary's center of gravity second. This is the essence of air power and, based on historical precedents, the reason for having centrally-controlled air forces. Without the guidance of air power theory it is difficult if not impossible to develop enduring and practical vision, mission, and doctrinal statements. These elements, in turn, are essential to providing clear strategic direction for the air force. Without the development of air power theory, the air force will likely lack the cohesion and focus to operate in the new millennium.

Notes

1. Carl Builder, *The Icarus Syndrome: The Role of Air Power Theory in the Evolution of the Us Air Force* (London: Transaction, 1994), p. xiii.
2. *Canadian Military Aerospace Power* - Volume 3.
3. Builder, *The Icarus Syndrome*, p. 290.
4. *Canadian Military Aerospace Power* - Volume 3; *Out of the Sun: Aerospace Doctrine for the Canadian Forces* (Winnipeg: Graig Kelman & Associates Ltd), pp 19-22.; and *USAF Basic Doctrine* (September 1997), pp 21-35.
5. Builder, *The Icarus Syndrome*, p. 287.
6. Ed J.B. Sykes, *The Concise Oxford Dictionary of Current English 7th Edition* (New York: Oxford University Press, 1984), p. 1109.
7. Builder, *The Icarus Syndrome*, p. 206.
8. Harold R. Winton, "A Black Hole in the Wild Blue Yonder: The Need for a Comprehensive Theory of Air Power", *Air Power History,* Vol 39 (Winter 1992), p. 32.
9. Sykes, *Oxford Dictionary,* p. 1200.
10. Builder, *The Icarus Syndrome,* p. 206.
11. Sykes, *Oxford Dictionary*, p. 648.
12. Builder, *The Icarus Syndrome,* p. 206.
13. Sykes, *Oxford Dictionary*, p. 283.
14. *Out of the Sun,* p. 1.
15. Builder, *The Icarus Syndrome*, p. 206.
16. Richard P. Hallion, *Doctrine, Technology, and Airwarfare; A Late Twentieth-Century Perspective,* Speech Extract, March 1987.
17. Builder, *The Icarus Agenda*, p. 230.
18. Scott Robertson, "The Development of Royal Air Force Strategic Bombing Doctrine between the Wars - A Revolution in Military Affairs?" *Air Power Journal,* Vol. XII, No. 1 (Spring 1998)
19. Royal Air Force, *Air Power Doctrine , AP 3000 - 2nd Edition*, Chief of the Air Staff, 1993; and Australian Defence Force, *The Air Power Manual,* March 1998
20. Brett Cairns, *Canadian Military Aerospace Power*, Volume 4 (1996), p. 87.
21. Builder, *The Icarus Agenda,* p. xiii.
22. I.B. Holley, "Reflections on the Search for Airpower Theory", *The Paths of Heaven: The Evolution of Air Power Theory*, (Maxwell AFB: Air University Press, 1997), p. 597.
23. Carl Von Clausewitz, *On War* (Random House, 1943), p. 578.
24. Winton, "A Black Hole in the Wild Blue Yonder", p. 42.
25. Builder, *The Icarus Agenda*, p. 230.
26. W.A.B. Douglas, *The Creation of a National Air Force: The Official History of the Royal Canadian Air Force*, Volume II (Minister of Supply and service Canada, 1986), pp. 140-143.
27. Cairns, *Canadian Military Aerospace Power*, p. xviii.
28. Colin Gibson, Air Power In Canada, May 1943, p 6.
29. Cairns, *Canadian Military Aerospace Power*, p. xxi.

30. John Treddenic, *Issues in Defence Management*, (Kingston: Queen's University Press, 1998), p. 65.
31. Cairns, *Canadian Military Aerospace Power*, p. xxii.
32. Glen Berg, *Scrambling for Dollars: Resource Allocation and the Politics of Canadian Fighter Aircraft Procurement 1943-1983*, (Kingston: Royal Military College of Canada, 1993), p 133.
33. Cairns, *Canadian Military Aerospace Power*, p. xxviii.
34. Berg, *Scrambling for Dollars*, p. 145.
35. Cairns, *Canadian Military Aerospace Power*, p. xxxi.
36. David Huddleston, *The Canadian Air Force Flight Plan: Old Wine New Bottles*, (Canadian Forces Command and Staff College, 1992), p. 6.
37. Ibid., p. 7.
38. National Defence, *Defence Planning Guidance 1998*, p 3.
39. Information synthesized from Winton, *The Black Hole in the Wild Blue Yonder; The Need for a Comprehensive Air Power Theory;* Builder, *The Icarus Syndrome; USAF Basic Doctrine;* Cairns, *Canadian Military Aerospace power; Out of the Sun*; and, Holley, "Reflections on the Search for Airpower Theory".
40. Cyberspace is defined as the electronic medium through which information flows.
41. Information synthesized from Winton, *The Black Hole in the Wild Blue Yonder; The Need for a Comprehensive Air Power Theory;* Builder, *The Icarus Syndrome; USAF Basic Doctrine;* Cairns, *Canadian Military Aerospace power; Out of the Sun*; and, Holley, "Reflections on the Search for Airpower Theory".
42. Canadian Forces College Maritime Component Program Naval Doctrine Manual, pp. 4-19.
43. Information synthesized from Winton, *The Black Hole in the Wild Blue Yonder; The Need for a Comprehensive Air Power Theory;* Builder, *The Icarus Syndrome; USAF Basic Doctrine;* Cairns, *Canadian Military Aerospace power; Out of the Sun*; and, Holley, "Reflections on the Search for Airpower Theory"
44. *The Manoeuverist Approach to Operations and Mission Command*, The Army Lessons Learned Centre Dispatches, Vol. 5, No. 1, March 1998 p. 11.
45. Information synthesized from John Warden, *The Air Campaign* (Washington: National Defence University Press, 1988).
46. National Defence, Chief of the Air Staff FY99/00 Business Plan, pp. 60-62.
47. Ibid., p. 7.
48. Bid., pp. 60-62.
49. Ibid., p 16.

AEROSPACE DOCTRINE

Lieutenant-Colonel Brian D. Wheeler, Major Donald Albert,
Major Mark Chinner, Major Michel Latouche,
Major Marian Miszkiel, LColonel Josée-Ann Paradis,
Major Jeff Whiddon, and Major Ross Wuerth

Any airforce which does not keep its doctrine ahead of its equipment and its vision far into the future can only delude the nation into a false sense of security.[1]

Robert Frank Futrell, 1989

Introduction

Based on the theory that air power could win wars, United States Air Force (USAF) doctrine used to focus on what needed to be done by air assets to accomplish this task regardless of the political constraints. However, a recent study of USAF doctrine reveals that the reliance on aerospace power theory as its underlying doctrinal belief was abandoned in favour of writing doctrine to be consistent with national policy and strategy.[2] The question remains: should doctrine be rooted by the theory of aerospace power and describe all theoretical capability or should it contain only those capabilities aligned with strategic and national policy?

Out of the Sun, the publication which outlines Canada's military aerospace doctrine, recognizes the distinction between aerospace power theory and national policy. It identifies the cornerstones of basic and operational-level doctrine as aerospace power theory and combat experience. *Out of the Sun* defines doctrine as fundamental truths similar to the principles of war that stand the test of time, while providing broad guidance on how forces can best be constituted, maintained and employed.[3] Canada has also removed national policy from basic and operational-level doctrine and relegated it to the correct place as strategic doctrine.

Aerospace power theory must continue to be the foundation of doctrine while national policy is necessary for shaping the operation.

Notwithstanding these facts, *Out of the Sun* requires revision to reflect current aerospace philosophy, concepts and operations. Accordingly, a thorough review and analysis of the book's contents was completed by the authors and compared to other existing doctrinal publications, including those of the USAF, RAF, and RAAF. A review of Canadian aerospace doctrinal literature from 1968 to the present, as well as selected foreign doctrine, was completed to determine what elements of aerospace operations should be included in a proposed doctrine. A comparison of these findings with the contents of *Out of the Sun* was made and resulted in recommendations for improving current Canadian Forces aerospace doctrine.

This paper commences with a look at a few basic definitions which were created from a compilation of existing definitions on aerospace power and doctrine. Next is a short historical discussion of the Canadian Operational-Level of Doctrine that looks at past doctrinal publications and puts into context the origins of *Out of the Sun* as Canada's current aerospace doctrine. Finally, a list of proposed topics for inclusion in a basic doctrine manual is presented, along with arguments to substantiate the need for their inclusion. In summary, because current basic aerospace doctrine requires revision, this paper will review the content of recent aerospace doctrinal material, including a critical analysis of *Out of the Sun*, and recommend an outline for future comprehensive Canadian Forces aerospace doctrine.

Basic Definitions and the Doctrinal Model

New definitions were created after the authors conducted a thorough review of previously published material on the subject of doctrine and aerospace power. A list of existing definitions that were examined, as well as their sources, can be found at Annex A. In the meantime, the following definitions should form the baseline for further doctrinal analysis and are recommended for inclusion in future aerospace doctrine:

Aerospace:

> All areas within the earth's atmosphere and outer space considered as a single region for the operation of defence weapons systems, aircraft and spacecraft; the study and investigation of this region.[4] It is the multi-dimensional operating environment wherein air forces can perform all of their missions.[5]

Aerospace Power:

> The projection of force, utilizing the full range of aerospace capabilities, both military and civilian, to achieve political and military objectives during wartime as well as in periods of tension, crisis, or in peacetime.

Aerospace Doctrine:

> The fundamental principles, theories, and proven practices which provide broad and enduring guidance for the application of aerospace power.

Purpose of Doctrine:

> To provide the foundation and framework for the organization, training, development, employment and sustainment of aerospace forces.

In order to properly understand doctrine one must first agree on definitions for the various levels of doctrine.

Strategic Doctrine - Strategic-Level Guidance:

> Strategic doctrine reflects national defence policy. It defines force capabilities, constraints and broad objectives in terms of military needs and foreign and economic policy of the nation.[6]

Joint Doctrine:

> Joint Doctrine describes the manner in which two or more services/environments carry out operations together.[7]

Combined Doctrine:

> Combined doctrine describes the best way to integrate and deploy aerospace forces with the forces of allies in coalition warfare. It establishes the principles, organization and fundamental procedures agreed upon between or among allied forces. Combined doctrine supports mutual defence treaties, agreements or organizations, and promotes compatible arrangements for the employment of armed forces in combined operations.[8]

Basic Aerospace Doctrine:

> Basic Aerospace Doctrine consists of fundamental principles and theories governing the proper use of assets in aerospace operations.[9]

Operational Aerospace Doctrine:

> Operational-Level Doctrine is developed from basic aerospace doctrine and consists of fundamental principles and theories governing the proper use of assets in the context of distinct objectives, force capabilities and operational environments. Unlike basic aerospace doctrine, the principles and theories of operational aerospace doctrine are dynamic and generally more detailed.[10]

Tactical Aerospace Doctrine:

> Tactical Aerospace Doctrine is developed from basic and operational doctrine, and describes in precise detail how specific systems should be operated, and assets employed, to achieve mission objectives.[11]

Figure 1, on the previous page, depicts the relationship between the various doctrinal levels. This paper focuses primarily on the basic and operational levels of aerospace doctrine.

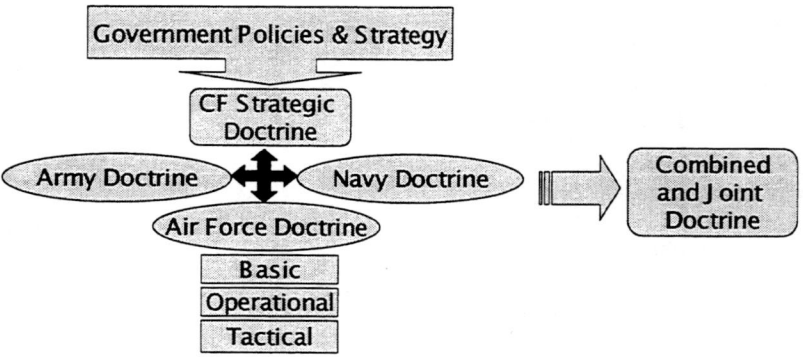

Figure 1. The levels of Doctrine

Figure 1, on the previous page, depicts the relationship between the various doctrinal levels. This paper focuses primarily on the basic and operational levels of aerospace doctrine.

The Canadian Operational Level of Doctrine

In reviewing the history of Canadian operational level doctrine three observations become evident. First, the re-organization of the nation's defence structure disrupts ownership and promotes a lack of transference of doctrinal issues. Second, small air forces may be prone to operating at the strategic and tactical levels due to a lack of major campaign planning experience. Third, given the above conditions, the tactical level will continue to develop tactical doctrine in response to changing necessities regardless of the existence of operational doctrine.

Before the unification of the three services in 1968, the writing of aerospace doctrine was the purview of the RCAF. In 1984 Colonel P.J. Taggart wrote that the "unification of the services ... eliminated the processes and institutions which produced air force doctrine."[12] During the seven years between unification and the institutionalizing of Air Command, the Chief of Air Doctrine and Operations maintained jurisdiction over air doctrine. Throughout this period, the air arms of the Royal Canadian Navy and the Canadian Army retained their airframe-dependent publications while awaiting a consolidation of the doctrine under the yet-to-be-formed Air Command.

Colonel Taggert further suggested that a doctrinal vacuum continued to exist even after 1975 due to a "certain amount of tension and friction" between Air Command and the Chief of Air Doctrine and Operations as to ownership of Canadian operational-level doctrine.[13] The solution at the time was the development and issue of *The Manual of Air Doctrine* (CFP 283) and the *Air Force Operational Development Guide* (AFODG)[14]. Despite a renewed focus on air doctrine issues, the content of CFP 283 was similar to *Out of the Sun* in that it contained basic-level doctrine. This pan-air force description omitted the necessary detail required at the operational level. Thus the lack of ownership or transference between pre-unification doctrine manuals and the issue of CFP 283 resulted in a loss of detail in operational doctrine. While the need for detail still existed, it filtered down to the tactical-level in various tactical instruction manuals where it would remain until 1989.

This was a classic example of a small air force confining itself to basic- and tactical-level doctrine. Squadron Leader S.A. Mackenzie of the Royal New Zealand Air Force (RNZAF) decribed the situation thus:

> Although small air forces will have command levels equating to tactical, operational, and strategic operations, it is likely that most small air forces effectively operate at only two levels: tactical and strategic. A scarcity of doctrine at the operational level of war and the lack of air campaign planning experience often results in strategic-level doctrine and thinking collapsing down on the tactical-level.[15]

This methodology sufficed for Canada, as the country had few occasions before 1989 to participate in coalition operations. If operational-level doctrine was required, CF personnel would need to rely on basic- and tactical-level doctrine for application to the situation.

With the realization that coalition operations would be the most likely future for the CF, and following the 1989 air symposium, the CDS directed an *ad hoc* committee to consolidate the operational-level doctrine scattered in over fifty tactical publications.[16] In 1989, the B-GA 400 series of publications gave the Canadian Air Force operational-level doctrine that replaced not only the CFP 283 for basic doctrine, but also detailed task-specific operational doctrine previously found in lower-level publications. The structure of the set of B-GA-400 series publications included an overarching volume entitled *Basic Aerospace Doctrine*, while the subset volumes included Group-specific operational doctrines for the fighter, transport, maritime, tactical helicopter, and search-and-rescue communities.

A recent look at the CF documentation database and a review of all B-GA 400 series publications revealed that the last update to any of the publications was issued in 1994. The exact date of discontinuation that the B-GA 400 series is unknown as the CF publication database only lists these documents as "inactive".[17] While *Out of the Sun* does not have a date of issue, it could be presumed that this book was written to replace the B-GA 400 series. The dissolution of the various Air Groups on 31 July 1997, further complicated the situation in that all Group documentation, orders, and directives needed to be consolidated under the authority of the newly-formed 1 Canadian Air Division (1 CAD). The tremendous scope of this project necessitated that priority be given to the issuance of 1 CAD orders. Consequently, *Out of the Sun* reflects some dated topics that will be discussed later in this paper.

Proposed Model for Basic Aerospace Doctrine

Past and current doctrinal publications were reviewed and compared against the content of *Out of the Sun* in order to provide recommendations for an outline to future comprehensive Canadian Forces aerospace doctrine. The doctrinal topics covered in *Out of the Sun* are generally quite acceptable and all-encompassing; however, some modification is required. Recommended changes to the contents are presented below. These range from minor changes of focus to more significant revisions, such as expanding the impact of space operations and information operations, and significantly reducing the level of detail on sustainment operations. Table 1 lists the topics which should be included in a revised Canadian basic aerospace doctrinal manual.

Military Doctrine Model
War and the Principles of War
Aerospace Power and the Principles of Aerospace Power at War
Command and Control
The Air Component / Joint Elements
Combat Aerospace Operations
Supporting Operations
Sustainment Operations and Force Generation
Information Operations

Table 1. Topics for inclusion in a Revised *Basic* Aerospace Doctrinal Manual

Military Doctrine

In his paper, *Air Power Doctrine Revisited*, Alan Stephens argues that "[t]he absence from a particular air force's order of battle of the capability to conduct one or more of the roles does not...invalidate the doctrinal relevance of that role, it simply means that, for certain reasons, the decision has been made to do without it."[18] *Out of the Sun* clearly embraces this important concept by including roles such as electronic warfare, and capabilities such as tactical reconnaissance, that are not possessed by Canada. Unfortunately, *Out of the Sun's* definition of aerospace doctrine is too narrow and would gain in clarity by including a discussion of this concept.

While not a contradiction to the previous point, basic aerospace doctrine should also serve as an instrument to support the acquisition of new capabilities. In order to do this, it is important that the doctrine identify fundamental requirements that will help ensure that an aerospace force is properly manned, equipped, trained and supported. For example, the NATO doctrine for tactical air operations identifies eight requirements as they apply to aerospace power. These apply to Canada's basic aerospace doctrine and therefore should be included within the appropriate manual along with those fundamental requirements already set forth in *Out of the Sun*. The NATO requirements are:

Interoperability:

> In the wider sense, it is the critical ability of all elements of aerospace power to work and interact in harmony.

Sustained operations:

> Aerospace forces should be able to operate effectively over prolonged periods.

Operations in hostile electronic environment:

> Aerospace forces should be capable of operating in a hostile electronic environment.

Survival to operate:

> Through the use of passive and active measures, aerospace forces should the capability to survive enemy attacks.

Operations in all conditions of light and weather:

> Aerospace forces should be capable of operating in all light and weather conditions.

Readiness:

> Forces should be capable of timely responses to enemy attacks.

Training:

> Forces should be trained the way they are expected to fight.

Communications:

> Communications should satisfy the aerospace power operational

needs.[19]

In addition to the above, it would be appropriate to include several basic definitions within the "Military Doctrine" section of a basic aerospace doctrine manual, including the following from Colonel Brett Cairns:

> Military operations require the application of military power to achieve operational and strategic objectives and can range from war to a variety of operations other than war (OOTW). Canada's air force is the component of the CF that can bring aerospace power to bear as part of a military operation.[20]

Although some manuals, including *Out of the Sun*, insert stand-alone historical commentaries throughout, these historical references should be made only to illustrate a principle or concept of doctrine. Although such commentary may be appropriate within a historical air power publication, it should not be included in a doctrinal manual unless a separate chapter on the history of Canadian doctrine is deemed appropriate.

Finally, it is interesting to note that the writings of Clausewitz have not influenced Canadian military doctrinal writings as they have in the United States. There appears "to be an absence in Canada of a rigorous approach to the study of warfare in the professional education system of the officer corps"[21]. Consequently, the important concept of educating CF members using doctrinal concepts should also be addressed in the "Military Doctrine" section.

War and the Principles of War

Out of the Sun discusses at length the characteristics, nature, categories, principles and levels of war. Not all of this information need be included in basic-level aerospace doctrine because much of it lies above the basic level. However, it is useful background information to set the stage for a discussion on aerospace doctrine and provides a link to higher levels of doctrine. Of particular interest to the new student of doctrine will be a section that describes the levels of war, operational art and the spectrum of conflict. These must be included in any basic aerospace doctrine manual and are defined below.

Levels of War:

Three levels of war link strategic objectives to the tactical operations of combat forces. These are strategic, operational, and tactical:

Strategic Level:

The level of war at which a nation or group of nations determines national or multinational (alliance or coalition) security objectives and guidance, and develops and uses national resources to accomplish those objectives.

Operational Level:

The level of war at which campaigns and major military operations are planned, conducted and sustained to accomplish strategic objectives within theatres or areas of operations.

Tactical Level:

The level of war at which battles and engagements are planned and executed to accomplish military objectives assigned to tactical units or task forces.[22]

Operational Art:

Operational art occurs at the level that links tactical action to strategic objectives. It translates the commander's strategy (or intent) into operational design, and ultimately tactical action, by orchestrating the key activities of all levels of war.[23]

The Spectrum of Conflict:

Relations between different peoples exist in a condition either of peace or of conflict. Peace exists when there is an absence of violence or the threat of violence. Conflict exists when violence is either manifested or threatened. The object of conflict is to impose one's will upon the enemy. The means to that end is the coordinated employment of the various instruments of national power including diplomatic, economic and political efforts as well as the application or threat of violence by military force. The spectrum of conflict (Figure 2) describes the varying states of relations between nations or groups and the continuum of operations relates to the range of military responses to peace and conflict, including war.

In conflicts that have proven resistant to both peacemaking and peace enforcement efforts, there may be no alternative but to transition to war. War is essentially a subset of conflict and not an isolated state. As with peace and conflict, the distinction between conflict other-than-war and war will be blurred because a conflict may encompass a period of war-fighting and then transition to prosecution through other means. This 'transitional haze' from peace to war is illustrated in Figure 2.

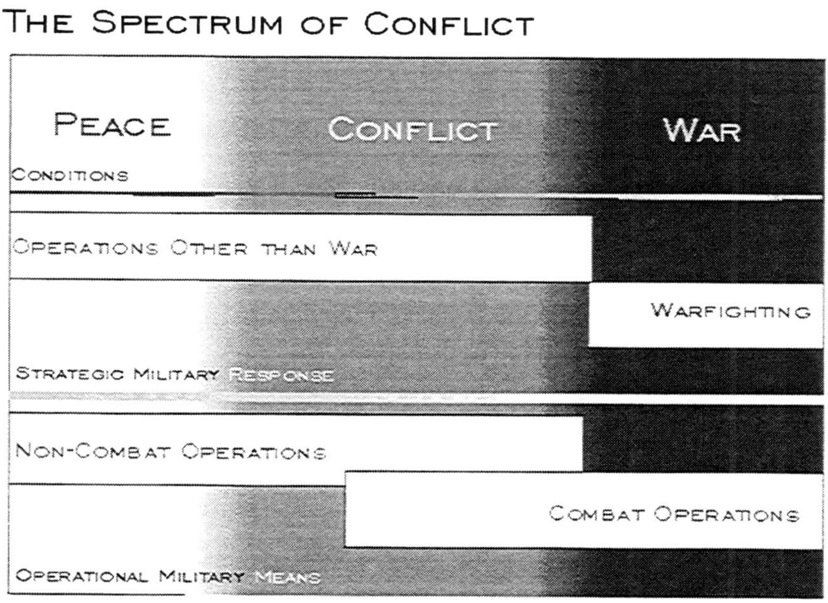

THE SPECTRUM OF CONFLICT

PEACE	CONFLICT	WAR
CONDITIONS		
OPERATIONS OTHER THAN WAR		WARFIGHTING
STRATEGIC MILITARY RESPONSE		
NON-COMBAT OPERATIONS		COMBAT OPERATIONS
OPERATIONAL MILITARY MEANS		

Figure 2. The Spectrum of Conflict [24]

A nation is a force generator in its own right. This ability is reflected through its 'elements of national power'. It is recommended that an overview of the elements, which include politics, demographics, economy and military, be added to the introductory chapter of an aerospace doctrine manual.

Aerospace Power and the Principles of Aerospace Power at War

Although the word "aerospace" is appropriately used in this section of *Out of the Sun*, it is not consistently applied throughout the manual. In its place, one sometimes finds the old word "air". It is recommended that the term "aerospace" be used throughout any aerospace doctrine manual.

Out of the Sun includes a brief chapter to introduce and define the different components of aerospace power. Although appropriate, the section is inconsistent and generates confusion in its use of the term "aerospace". Consequently, the hierarchy of aerospace operations detailed in Chapter 5 of *Out of the Sun* should include an "aerospace strategy" defined as the "overall employment plan for [aerospace] forces in war."[25] This would be followed by "aerospace campaigns" or "sub-campaigns", themselves defined as a "coordinated series of major [aerospace] operations or sub-campaigns, designed to achieve a specific strategic objective."[26] As well, an aerospace sub-campaign should include either a "counter-aerospace action" instead of "counter-air action", or introduce an additional category of action, perhaps called "counter-space action". As shown in Figure 3, the third level of the hierarchy should be "aerospace operations" and should include "combat aerospace operations", "supporting aerospace operations" and "sustainment operations".

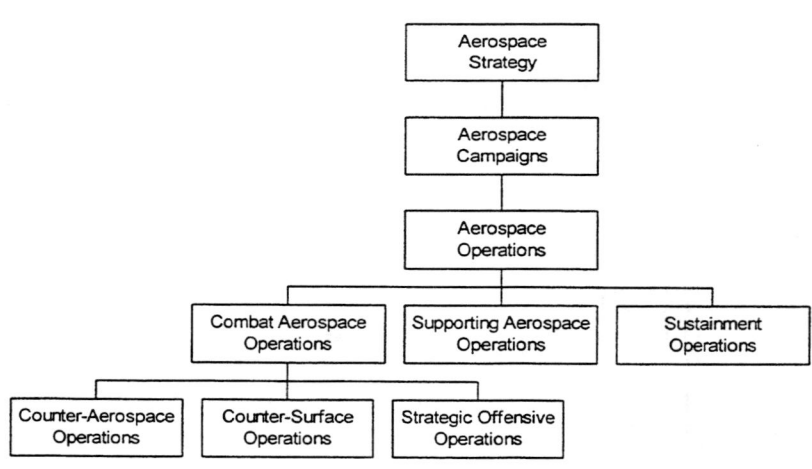

Figure 3. Aerospace Operations[27]

A discussion of "Combat Power" would be suitable for inclusion in a basic aerospace doctrine manual. Combat power can be applied by

Aerospace Doctrine 153

the sea, land, and aerospace components of a military force through the prosecution of campaigns, operations, battles and engagements, as defined below:

Campaigns:

> A series of related major military operations aimed at accomplishing strategic or operational objectives.

Operations:

> Military actions needed to gain the objectives of a campaign.

Battles:

> A set of related engagements that could affect the course of a campaign.

Engagements:

> Tactical actions fought between small forces that are limited in area and duration.[28]

The blending of air, space, land, sea and sub-surface "battlefields" with "jointness" and technology has resulted in the emergence of a "battlespace". This is supported by CFP (J)5(4), CF Joint Doctrine, and its vision of geomatics[29] support of terrain/space visualization for the Joint Task Force Commander (JTFC). Similarly, the Air Component Commander (ACC) of an operation must know the details of all the elements that he/she is supporting or that the air campaign is restricted to in the operational-level battlespace. Cyberspace and the aspects of information operations can also be conceptually linked to the battlespace.

Command and Control

Out of the Sun provides a brief introductory discussion of command and control in the chapter, *Command and Control of Aerospace Forces*. It is recommended that reference to the command and control of space operations and military space assets be briefly included within such a command and control (C^2) definition.

Out of the Sun provides a supplemental section to its chapter on

Command and Control of Aerospace Forces. This section contains detailed guidelines for the preparation of an "Estimate of the Situation" and the "Air Campaign Plan". These two processes and their related documents are not part of aerospace doctrine, and therefore do not belong in the main body of such a manual. As was rightly pointed out by LCol Dennis Margueratt:

> [T]he detailed description of the planning staff should not be contained in a doctrine manual. This is one of the failings of *Out of the Sun* - it tries to address issues that are better suited to standard operating procedures than to doctrine. Having said that, the description of the AOC [Air Operations Centre] in *Out of the Sun* is contradictory.[30]

However, both of these processes are described in detail in other Canadian Forces manuals. Therefore, it would be appropriate to simply make reference to these manuals along with the Air Force Operational Planning Process AFOPP - ACP(2) which is currently in use and envisaged for the future of 1 Canadian Air Division (1CAD) and the Chief of the Air Staff (CAS).

All the remaining material on the *Command and Control of Aerospace Forces* found within *Out of the Sun* should be included within a manual on basic aerospace doctrine.

The Air Component and its Joint Elements

Out of the Sun provides an excellent overview of the Air Component and its various parts. However, there is very little mention of joint or combined operations. Canadian aerospace forces will likely be part of a joint and/or combined operation. A link with the CF joint doctrine is therefore required to provide a realistic and complete understanding of the Air Component within the Joint Task Force (JTF) under the Joint Force Air Component Commander (JFACC).

The Canadian Forces are a unified force that must espouse its "jointness" throughout its doctrine. *Out of the Sun* limits its reference to CF Joint Doctrine CFP (J)5(4) to a very short paragraph (103b). It is recommended that the extracts included in Annex B to this paper, and the intent of Joint Doctrine promulgated in CFP (J)5(4), be quoted or summarized to further the utility and CF application of its Air Doctrine. Reference to the terminology being employed today and for the near future must be reflected. This includes CFOPP, JPITL, JAOC, JGAI, JFACC etc.

It must be emphasized that air force targeting must be planned and executed using the AFOPP, the Joint Priority Integrated Targeting List (JPITL), Air Tasking Orders (ATOs) and be executed and governed by the Law of Armed Conflict.

Since there is a requirement for "jointness", it is necessary to write aerospace doctrine, as well as the doctrine of the land and sea elements, because "joint doctrine can only be developed as a consequence of first having enunciated single service doctrine as a basis."[31]

Combat Aerospace Operations

As addressed earlier and shown in Figure 3, combat aerospace operations should be expanded to include the space dimension of modern warfare. Additionally, *Out of the Sun* discusses the subject of strategic aerospace defence operations almost as an after-thought to defensive counter-air operations. As seen during the Gulf War, space played a significant if not a major contributing role in the successful outcome of the war. Space-based and ground-based sensors of US Space Command (USSPACECOM), traditionally used only for strategic aerospace defence of North America, were used to warn the JTF of incoming Iraqi Scud missile attacks. While there were other examples of the use of space in the Gulf War, the point is that space is now a critical component of warfare. Consequently, it would follow that strategic aerospace defence operations could either be defined as a separate role or include the "air" aspect of strategic aerospace defence in the current defensive counter-air role. The space portion would change "defensive counter-space" to "counter-space". The latter is favoured because, doctrinally, the concept of aerospace warfare should be true whether or not it is for the defence of a nation's heartland or for a conflict abroad.

Canadian Air Doctrine does not clearly address the recent use of space, its assets and DND policy in a clear manner in *Out of the Sun*. Joint doctrine identifies *Space Operations*[32] and this must be included in Aerospace Doctrine. In recent years, space has emerged as an increasingly important component of the global security environment. Space already supports the traditional military activities of the maritime, land, and air forces, including command, control and communications, intelligence-gathering, surveillance, navigation, mapping, meteorological services and arms control verification. With the advent of missile warfare, the role of space in protecting the modern nation-state has taken on added significance.

Out of the Sun states that "aerospace is the total expanse of the air and space above the earth's surface. It is the multi-dimensional operating environment wherein air forces can perform all of their missions."[33] Consequently, space is an element of air power since *Out of the Sun* states that "aerospace power is considered to be the capability to use platforms for military purposes operating in, or passing through the aerospace."[34]

Freedom of Action

Conceptually, the freedom of action an aerospace power wants to have during an aerospace campaign may also be influenced by the freedom of action of other, either sequential or parallel, campaigns. In other words, it is possible that there could be within a given theatre different degrees of control for each campaign (aerospace, ground, sea and information) – any one of these having an impact on the aerospace power's freedom of action.[35] While beyond the scope of this paper, the concept of "Theatre Control," (see Figure 4) should be explored further for possible inclusion in future basic-level aerospace doctrine.

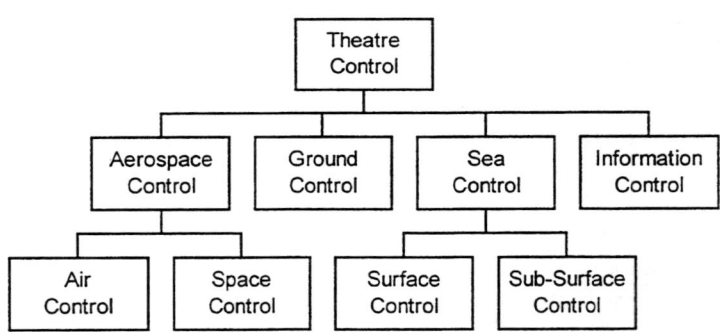

Figure 4. Theatre Freedom of Action

Strategic Offensive Operations

Out of the Sun states that these operations are aimed at the enemy's strategic centres of gravity. These include political, industrial, military, and economic power bases.[36] Besides stating that "target sets must be selected carefully,"[37] the document provides too little guidance about targeting considerations. One commentator, Air Vice-Marshal Mason, RAAF, claims that a "new aerospace paradigm for the 21st Century" is required and that a "re-evaluation of the way we do business" is relevant to small and large air forces alike.[38] He argues that the concept of strategic [attack] needs to be re-thought because potential adversaries have learned from the mistakes of Saddam Hussein in that they will try to "evade the traditional battlefield, preferring instead to rely on dispersal, deception, concealment and mobility, especially of surface-to-air missiles (SAMs), medium range ballistic missiles (MRBMs), and command, control, communications and intelligence (C^3I)."[39] In his view, "'strategic' air attack...should be more accurately defined, not by the aircraft or weapons, nor by the distance covered, nor even by the nature of the target, but by the direct relationship of a target to the overall political objective."[40] AVM Mason also suggests that it is important to re-evaluate the targeting process. He opines that attacks on industrial and economic infrastructure "should take into account considerations of post rehabilitation and reconstruction,"[41] that morale and willpower are "elusive targets", and that there it is little historical justification for exerting pressure on an enemy's government by conducting attacks aimed at weakening its population's morale.[42]

Combat Aerospace Operations

As noted in the next section, Offensive Counter-Air (OCA) Operations must be twinned with Counter-Space Operations to form a new, broadly-based activity which we have called Counter Aerospace Operations. These two sub-topics are discussed below.

Offensive Counter-Air Operations

The three roles, as defined by *Out of the Sun*, under OCA operations are: "airfield attack", "fighter sweep" and "Suppression of Enemy Air Defences" (SEAD).[43] A closer analysis reveals the role of "airfield attack" is too restrictive. The definition of airfield attack should be changed to reflect the fact that airfields are not necessarily static or change the name of the role, as per ATP-33(B), to counter-air attack.[44]

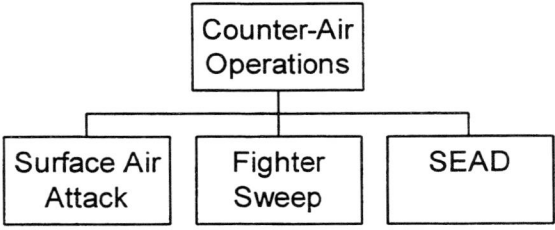

Figure 5. Counter-Air Operations

Counter-Space Operations

As suggested earlier, if we desire to pursue the use of the term "aerospace" in our doctrine to its logical extension, then we should include counter-aerospace operations in space. Space plays a large part in modern warfare and therefore consideration should be given to include this dimension to a much greater extent in our doctrine. Space doctrine, similar to counter-air operations, should include Offensive Counter-Space (OCS) and Defensive Counter-Space (DCS) operations under the umbrella of counter-space operations.[45] OCS operations are "operations [to] destroy, neutralize an adversary's space systems or the information they provide at a time and place of [their] choosing through attacks on the space, terrestrial or link elements of space systems."[46] For that purpose, OCS operations use "lethal or nonlethal [sic] means to achieve five major purposes: deception, disruption, denial, degradation, and destruction of space assets and capabilities."[47] On the other hand, the DCS operations "consist of active and passive actions to protect [their] space-related capabilities from enemy attack or interference."[48] DCS operations are further sub-divided into active and passive defences. Active defence seeks to "detect, track, identify, intercept, and destroy or neutralize enemy space and missile forces," while passive defence wants to "reduce the vulnerabilities and to protect and increase the survivability of friendly space forces and the information they provide."[49]

Counter-Surface (Joint) Operations

It is apparent that Canada wanted to follow the USAF lead by removing Battlefield Air Interdiction (BAI) as a mission under tactical air operations from its basic doctrine. However, when *Out of the Sun* explains the roles of air/land (tactical air) operations, it stills refers to "offensive air support" and still includes BAI.[50] If we intend to remove it from our doctrine, then it should be removed completely. In regards to air/sea (maritime air) operations, *Out of the Sun* declares that these operations "may be considered under two broad categories: direct support and area or associated support operations."[51] Unfortunately, when the doctrine further defines "area operations", it mistakenly uses the term "air operations."[52] Further, when describing TASMO (Tactical Air Support for Maritime Operations), *Out of the Sun* identifies "associate support" operations as a separate role to area operations.[53]

As shown in Figure 6, it is our opinion that *Out of the Sun* should adopt the concept of counter-space operations similar to the USAF. Further, the ambiguity regarding BAI and offensive air support needs to be

Aerospace Doctrine 159

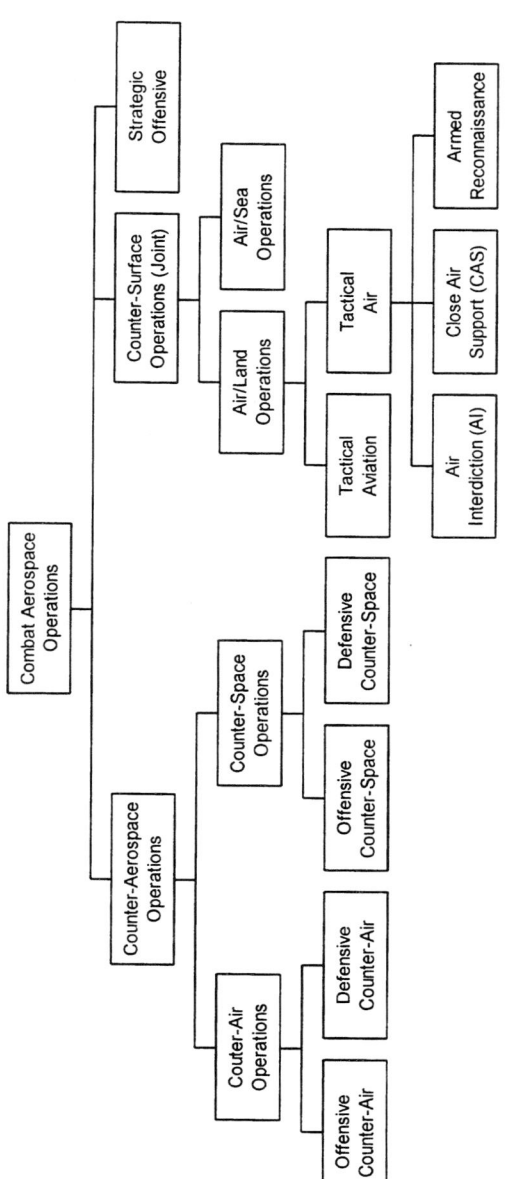

Figure 6. Combat Aerospace Operations

corrected by removing any reference to them in the document. Finally, *Out of the Sun* is inconsistent in the type of categories of maritime air operations and should amend them accordingly.

Nuclear Aerospace Doctrine

The development and use of nuclear weapons, along with the application of these weapons systems for nuclear deterrence, has had a definite impact on aerospace doctrine. The interaction between the Canadian Forces and nations that possess nuclear weapons is a matter for strategic aerospace doctrine based on political direction from the federal government. Reference to this fact needs to be made within a basic aerospace doctrine manual. Wording to this effect is provided within *Out of the Sun*. However, additional information should be included in basic aerospace doctrine to explain how the Canadian Forces would defend themselves against a nuclear attack and how the CF would interact with an allied force possessing nuclear weapons if ever required to be co-located with these forces.

Supporting Operations

As mentioned above, reference to "Supporting Air Operations" should be amended to read "Supporting Aerospace Operations". *Out of the Sun* tends to categorize all flying assets as "support" if it is anticipated that they will not enter into one-on-one offensive combat with the enemy. However, we believe that operational assets such as tactical air transport and AWACS operations are integral to the air and land battles. Accordingly, they must be classified as operational rather than support, regardless of whether they are involved with lethal or non-lethal combat. If such assets or activities are deemed to be "only" indirect-support, then the commander being supported has no authority to move the operating location of the aerospace assets. On the other hand, the operational commander will have direct control over those aerospace assets integrally involved with the tactical operation. Therefore, it is recommended that the categorization of aerospace assets as "Support" versus "Operational", as described within *Out of the Sun*, be studied further.

Air "Escort" activities are discussed in *Out of the Sun* in the section dealing with DCA. However, "escort" can also be OCA as well as participating in a support role. In the sub-section dealing with Aerospace Surveillance and Reconnaissance, *Out of the Sun* only makes a one-word mention of space-based sensors. Today, space assets can play a very significant wartime role in the areas of surveillance, reconnaissance and communications. Therefore, a much more detailed assessment of the impact of space assets on these areas should be made

Lastly, regarding Support Operations, the subject of "Intelligence" Operations is included within the chapter on sustainment operations. Since "Int-Ops" is usually intricately involved with aerospace operations, such activities are more appropriately kept within a discussion of aerospace "Support" Operations. Additional comments regarding the subject of Supporting Operations can be found at Annex C to this paper.

Sustainment Operations and Force Generation

Sustainment is important and is worthy of inclusion in any basic aerospace doctrine manual. However, the discussion should be limited to a brief operational-level overview about how sustainment operations directly support aerospace training activity and deployed operations. For example, an explanation of how the Canadian Forces Supply System will prepare for, and then support deployed aerospace operations is quite important. What is not required in a basic aerospace doctrine manual is a detailed section-by-section explanation of traditional in-Canada main operating base (MOB) sustainment activities. It is recommended that within a discussion of Aerospace Sustainment Operations, mention should be made to the new "Contingency Capability Concept" or "Triple C" that is now under development by members of the logistics staff within the office of the Chief of the Air Staff at National Defence Headquarters.

Prior to the detailed chapter on sustainment, *Out of the Sun* provides a very brief chapter about preparing aerospace forces for war, including discussions on personnel, organizational structures, equipment, and sustainment. This is "force generation" information and is suitable for inclusion in an aerospace doctrine manual. However, the concepts of sustainment and force generation can be merged together into one comprehensive chapter.

Information Operations

Canadian Forces Basic Aerospace Doctrine needs to include current theories, practices, and policies of information operations. Dominating the information spectrum is now as critical to all spectrums of conflict as controlling air and space. It is seen as an indispensable and synergistic component of air and space power. The US Air Force Basic Doctrine Manual 1-1 defines information superiority as "the ability to collect, control, exploit, and defend information while denying an adversary the ability to do the same and, like air and space superiority, includes gaining control over the information realm and fully exploiting military information functions."[54] The USAF information operations doctrine provides a good foundation on which to build a Canadian information operations doctrine.

Basic information operations doctrine for Canadian aerospace forces should address both its offensive and defensive nature. Offensive information operations are intended to deny, destroy, corrupt, or otherwise manipulate an adversary's information systems and command and control.[55] Offensive information operations attack an adversary's information and information systems by both kinetic and non-kinetic means. Defensive information operations provide operational security and guarantee access to our own information and information systems.

Out of the Sun states that, along with sea and land powers, "aerospace power is one of the three components of national military power."[56] This statement is true but it is too narrowly focused on the three traditional arms. It omits a very important facet of modern warfighting: information. Since no single service holds a dominant role in information, it should be viewed as a separate component of national military power. Consequently, as shown at Figure 7, doctrinally, warfighting should be composed of four rather than three campaigns. "Information", as a distinct campaign, should be fought jointly with the aerospace, land and maritime campaigns. The introduction to concepts of Information Operations[57] must be provided.

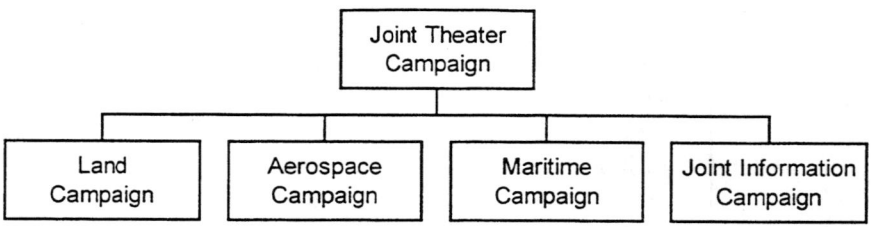

Figure 7. Warfare Campaigns

Inclusion of information operations into basic Canadian aerospace doctrine emphasizes that one of the commander's primary tasks is to gain and maintain information superiority. The objective is to achieve faster and more effective decision-making and command and control of his/her assigned forces than that of the adversary.[58]

Other Changes to the Manual

Information on the Law of Armed Conflict (LOAC) should be added as an annex to the basic aerospace doctrine for ease of reference. Several of the texts reviewed included the topics of LOAC and Rules of Engagement (ROE) within manuals of aerospace doctrine. These directly impact upon the application of air power and deserve mention within the main body of any basic aerospace doctrine manual. However, detailed discussion on these subjects should be reserved for an annex to the manual or a stand-alone publication.

Similarly, some manuals expound upon the doctrine creation process. It is suggested that the doctrinal process could be either be discussed as an annex to the basic aerospace doctrine manual, or via reference to a separate manual, thus keeping the main body of the manual focused on doctrinal issues. Lastly, *Out of the Sun* should be translated and published as an official DND publication and should include a glossary of definitions and a proper index.

Conclusion

A review of recent aerospace doctrinal literature, including a critical analysis of *Out of the Sun*, was completed to determine recommendations for improvement to current Canadian Forces aerospace doctrine. Although *Out of the Sun* was created to fill a doctrinal gap and provide Canada's air force with much-needed guidance on basic aerospace doctrinal matters, it requires revision to reflect current aerospace philosophy, concepts and operations.

Aerospace doctrine must be written in accordance with national defence policy and it must state the means to accomplish national and departmental goals. *Out of the Sun* recognizes the distinction between aerospace power and aerospace doctrine, and is not based on Canada's current technical aerospace capabilities and national policy. However, the document tends to delve into areas other than those required in a basic doctrinal manual. For example, the level of information provided on Sustainment Operations goes well beyond that which is needed in basic doctrine. Similarly, there is no requirement for an entire section on Planning Process at this level. On the other hand, some of the information required in today's basic doctrine is absent from the manual. *Out of the Sun* should be modified to include elements such as space operations and information operations. Furthermore, some of the terminology used and concepts described need to be modified to better complement today's doctrinal realities.

Finally, along with a basic aerospace doctrine publication, there is a need to revive the operational-level doctrinal manuals that were abandoned as a result of the recent disbanding of the Air Groups.

Notes

1. Robert Frank Futrell, *Ideas, Concepts, Doctrine: Basic Thinking in the United States Airforce*, Vol I, 1907-1960, (Maxwell Air Force Base: Air University Press, 1989), p. 180.
2. Dr James A. Mowbray, "Air Force Doctrine Problems: 1926-Present," *AIRPOWER Journal*, (Winter 1995), p. 22.
3. Canadian Forces, *Out of the Sun* (Winnipeg: Craig Kelman & Associates Ltd, undated, p. 3.
4. Definition of *aerospace* derived and modified from the that provided in *Funk & Wagnalls Standard College Dictionary*, (Funk & Wagnalls Publishing Company Inc, 1968).
5. Canadian Forces, *Out of the Sun* (Winnipeg: Craig Kelman & Associates Ltd, undated, p. 19.
6. Canadian Forces, B-GA 400, *Basic Aerospace Doctrine*.
7. Canadian Forces, *Out of the Sun* (Winnipeg: Craig Kelman & Associates Ltd, undated), p 3. As well, note: CF Joint Doctrine is promulgated in CFP (J)5(4).
8. Ibid., p. 3.
9. Ibid.
10. Canadian Forces, B-GA 450, *Air Transport Operations*
11. Canadian Forces, *Out of the Sun* (Winnipeg: Craig Kelman & Associates Ltd, undated), p. 4.
12. Colonel P.J. Taggart (CF), *A Working Paper on Proposals for the Development and Dissemination of Air Force Doctrine,* in *Air Doctrine Symposium, Summary of Proceedings*, (Trenton, Ontario, January 24, 1994, unpublished symposium notes), p. 5.
13. Ibid.
14. Canadian Forces, *The Manual of Air Doctrine (CFP 283)*, and *Air Force Operational Development Guide (AFODG)*. Discussion in this section concerning the historical aspects of these publications and related doctrine comes from the personal knowledge of Major Mark Chinner, a Maritime air navigator and Canadian Forces College CSC 25 student.
15. Squadron Leader S.A. Mackenzie (RNZAF), *Strategic Air Power Doctrine for Small Air Forces* (Canberra: Air Power Studies Centre, RAAF Base Fairbairn, 1994), p. 43.
16. Colonel Brett Cairns, *Canadian Military Aerospace Power,* Unpublished - prepared for the Canadian Forces College for internal use, (May 1996), Vol 2, Section 235.
17. From the research and personal knowledge of Major Mark Chinner, Maritime ANAV, and Canadian Forces College CSC 25 student.
18. Alan Stephens, "Air Power Doctrine Revisited," Paper Number 44: Royal Australian Air Force Air Power Studies Centre, (RAAF Base Fairbairn, May 1996), p. 29.
19. ATP-33(B), *NATO Tactical Air Doctrine*, (November 1986), p. 2-6 and 2-7.
20. Colonel Brett Cairns, *Canadian Military Aerospace Power,* Unpublished -

prepared for the Canadian Forces College for internal use, (May 1996), Vol 3, Section 302.
21. Lieutenant-Colonel Richard J. Young, "Clausewitz and His Influence on U. S. and Canadian Military Doctrine", in *The Changing Face of War*, ed. by Allan D. English, (Montreal & Kingston: McGill-Queen's University Press, 1998), p. 9.
22. Colonel Brett Cairns, *Canadian Military Aerospace Power*, Unpublished - prepared for the Canadian Forces College for internal use, (May 1996), Vol 3, Section 303.
23. Ibid., Vol 3, Sections 303 and 305.
24. Canadian Forces. B-GG-005-004/AF-000, *Canadian Forces Operations*, 1997-05-15, Chapter 1, Article 108, "The Spectrum of Conflict". May be found on the World Wide Web at http://www.dnd.ca/dcds/drs/pubs/cfdoc1_e.htm#108.
25. Canadian Forces, *Out of the Sun* (Winnipeg: Craig Kelman & Associates Ltd, undated, p. 32.
26. Ibid., p. 32.
27. Figure 3 introduces the term *aerospace* into hierarchical operational names. Thediagram was created using information and diagrams from Chapters 8 and 9 from the Canadian Forces publication *Out of the Sun*.
28. Colonel Brett Cairns, *Canadian Military Aerospace Power*, Unpublished - prepared for the Canadian Forces College for internal use, (May 1996), Vol 3, Section 306.
29. *Geomatics*, means "... those staff, scientific and engineering activities involved in the capture, storage, analysis, processing, presentation, dissemination and management of military geospatial information," as defined in DCDS/J2 Geomatics – CFP (J)5(4), *Defence Geomatics*.
30. From discussions with LCol Dennis Margueratt, Senior Air Staff Planner at Canadian Forces College, February 1999.
31. Squadron Leader S.A. Mackenzie (RNZAF), *Strategic Air Power Doctrine for Small Air Forces* (Canberra: Air Power Studies Centre, RAAF Base Fairbairn, 1994), p. 7.
32. Canadian Forces. B-GG-005-004/AF-000, *Canadian Forces Operations*, 1997-05-15, Chapter 26, *Space Operations*.
33. Canadian Forces, *Out of the Sun* (Winnipeg: Craig Kelman & Associates Ltd, undated, p. 19.
34. Ibid.
35. Alan Stephens, "Air Power Doctrine Revisited," Paper Number 44: Royal Australian Air Force Air Power Studies Centre, (RAAF Base Fairbairn, May 1996), p. 21-23. Alan Stephens expands the concept of theatre control to include air control, surface control (incorporating sub-surface control) and information control. He argues that they could be prosecuted separately, in parallel, or even ignored.
36. Canadian Forces, *Out of the Sun* (Winnipeg: Craig Kelman & Associates Ltd, undated, p. 77.

Aerospace Doctrine 167

37. Ibid., p 81 and 82. Strategic targets sets for conventional strategic aerospace attacks are: C^2 structures, key industries, transportation grids and enemy population.
38. Air Vice-Marshal Professor Tony Mason, "The Future of Air Power: Concepts of Operations," Paper Number 62: Royal Australian Air Force Air Power Studies Centre, (RAAF Base Fairbairn, March 1998), p. 1.
39. Ibid., p. 5 and 6.
40. Ibid., p. 6.
41. Ibid.
42. Ibid., p. 12.
43. Canadian Forces, *Out of the Sun* (Winnipeg: Craig Kelman & Associates Ltd, undated, p. 66-67.
44. ATP-33(B), *NATO Tactical Air Doctrine*, November 1986, p. 4-2.
45. United States Air Force, *AFDD 2-2*, p. 8.
46. Ibid.
47. Ibid.
48. Ibid., p. 10.
49. Ibid.
50. Canadian Forces, *Out of the Sun* (Winnipeg: Craig Kelman & Associates Ltd, undated, p. 87.
51. Ibid., p. 94.
52. Ibid., p 94.
53. Ibid., p. 97.
54. United States Air Force, *Air Force Basic Doctrine, Air Force Doctrine Document 1*, Secretary of the Air Force, September 1997, p. 31.
55. Ibid., p. 31.
56. Canadian Forces, *Out of the Sun* (Winnipeg: Craig Kelman & Associates Ltd, undated, p. 19.
57. Canadian Forces, B-GG-005-004/AI-032 *Information Operations (Draft)*, 1998-04-15.
58. Ibid., p. 44.

Annex A

Definitions Referenced During the Preparation of this Paper

Definitions of Air Power

"The capability to use platforms for military purposes operating or passing through the aerospace."[1]

"The principal and all-important mission of air power, when its equipment permits, is the attack of those vital objectives in a nation's economic structure which will tend to paralyze the nation's ability to wage war and thus contribute directly to the attainment of the ultimate objective of war, namely, the disintegration of the hostile will to resist."[2]

"The full range of a nation's air capability, military and civilian, in peace as well as war. Air power includes more then just military assets."[3]

"The projection of force for a military purpose utilizing a platform sustained in third dimension. The platform may be manned or unmanned, and either military or civilian in origin."[4]

"Airpower is the ability to project military force by or from a platform in the third dimension above the surface of the earth."[5]

From the United States Air Force: "Aerospace power is characterized by seven tenets which are important guidelines and considerations for commanders in addition to principles of war. Those tenets describe how aerospace power can be used to achieve military objectives as follows: centralized control/decentralized execution; flexibility/versatility; priority; synergy; balance; concentration; and persistence."[6]

From the Royal Air Force: "Air power can be defined as the ability to use platforms operating in or passing through the air for military purposes."[7]

"The largely independent use of manned aircraft to obtain a quick, decisive, and overwhelming victory over the enemy."[8]

Definitions of Doctrine

"Doctrine comprises of principles, theories and policies accepted as valid and reliable, which offer military forces good chances for success when applied in periods of tension, crises, or war. . . . A compilation of the immutable truths about the employment of aerospace forces in warfighting that have withstood a test of time."[9]

"Basic doctrine establishes fundamental principles that describe and guide the proper use of aerospace forces in war. It is the foundation of all aerospace doctrine, provides broad, enduring guidance which should be used when deciding how airforce forces should be organized, trained, equipped, employed and sustained. It is the cornerstone and provides the framework from which the air force develops operational and tactical doctrine."[10]

"Our doctrine represents (or should represent) the apex of our thinking about the best ways to use air power. It is our theory of victory."[11]

"The beliefs or ideas, both written and unwritten, about air power."[12]

"What we believe is the best way to do something having considered our experiences and those of others. In an air power sense, doctrine is what we believe to be true about air power and the best way to operate an air force. Doctrine is authoritative, but requires judgement in application."[13]

"Doctrine is at the heart of military activity. As the central body of beliefs about the conduct of war, it provides the guiding force for action, structure, organization and development. Doctrine represents the highest expression of a defence force's intellectual foundation. Doctrine should make clear why the organization is structured the way is it, what its objectives are, and in broad terms, how those objectives should be achieved."[14]

From the Royal Air force: "Doctrine is defined as an accumulation of knowledge which is gained primarily from the study and analysis of experience (what works best)."15

From the Royal Air Force: "Air power doctrine that set of principles which guide the use of air power in support of national or multinational defence objectives."16

From the Royal Australian Air Force: "The fundamental philosophy concerning the employment of a defence force, as the central body of beliefs which guides the application of combat power."17

"Doctrine is the official published viewpoint of a single military service or the Department of Defence as a whole, which describes how best to accomplish tactical, operational or strategic objectives, with military force."18

"Air Doctrine deals with the operations or aircraft whenever they operate and however they may be employed."19

From the United States Air Force, 1972: "The fundamental principles on the use of air power which form the central core of all air force doctrine."20

"Doctrine is subject to continual change as new developments, new experience, technological innovations, and the like, require us to reconsider and impel us towards a revised statement of official doctrine."21

Purpose of Doctrine

"We want doctrine to:

- reveal capabilities of air forces yet offer guidance on how best to use those capabilities
- be enduring yet flexible (i.e. be valid over time yet responsive to change)
- provide guidance to personnel yet remain open to interpretation
- provide direction yet not be too restrictive
- guide research and development yet adjust to new technological innovations; and
- set out maxims and imperatives"22

"Doctrine offers:

- a conceptual framework

- general guidance in specific situations
- a foundation for the air force (including force structure, strategy, tactics, training, and procedures)
- guidance for establishing employment priorities
- a sounding board for testing, evaluating, and employing new technologies and new policies; and
- a rationale for the organization and employment of air forces"[23]

"Military doctrine seeks primarily to influence the way in which military personnel think and it establishes a framework within which military operations can be understood."[24]

"Provides the foundation, the starting point, upon which every aspect of military activity is based. . . . Doctrine should provide a rationale for both organization and employment of military forces. Roles and missions should be determined from doctrine. It should also provide guidance in establishing priorities for procurement and it should act as a sounding board for testing and evaluating new concepts and policies."[25]

"Doctrine will not offer a definite solution to a specific problem. It will, however suggest the best course of action, to take given what we know of the past and that which we anticipate happening in the future. Doctrine acts as a compass indicating a general direction. It does not provide a detailed map. It guides the action, structure, and development of combat forces and what those forces should do in war and why. Doctrine is guidance and not procedure."[26]

"Doctrine also represents the mechanism through which all aspects of the air force's activities should be linked. It forms the basis from which planners will determine the best way to develop and employ that airforce's air power in the future. Finally, doctrine can act as a catalyst to initiate and guide research and development."[27]

"Doctrine is also a fundamental element in the development of future force structures and capability requirements."[28]

From the Royal Air Force: "Purpose is to advise and

guide; that is, it is not dogma and its application is not mandatory."[29]

"Military doctrine provides a conceptual framework for the development of policies and principles within which military forces guide their actions. Air force or aerospace doctrine is that branch of military doctrine or collection of fundamental principles which relates to the application of aerospace power."[30]

"Sound aerospace doctrine should provide a conceptual framework for policy formation, planning and procurement. Doctrine should be pervasive through all levels of military planning and operations."[31]

Annex B

Useful References from CF Joint Doctrine Manual CFP (J)5(4), Refering to "Air" and "Doctrine"

ARTICLE 114 - INTRODUCTION TO CF OPERATIONS

1. A CF Operation is defined as the employment of an element or elements of the CF to perform a specific mission. Certain CF operations are enhanced when environmental components operate in concert. Force entry operations provide good examples: **AIR**borne operations require land and **AIR** forces to be employed together; amphibious assaults may involve maritime, land and **AIR** forces. Other operations that are normally co-planned and conducted include PSYOPS, EW, C2W, intelligence, NBC defence, **AIR** defence, and peace support operations.

2. The CF is a unified force and, as a matter of routine, conducts operations involving elements of at least two environments. Notwithstanding the legal aspects of the NDA, which describes the CF as a single service, when elements of two or more environments of the CF are required to co-operate, they will do so under a joint structure, using internationally recognized joint terminology.

3. CF **DOCTRINE** must cater to both domestic and international operations without generating confusion within a Canadian force or amongst our allies, hence the use of joint terminology. In all cases, a commander will be named and appropriate elements will be assigned as required. C2 relationships will be based on the principles outlined in chapter 2 - Command and Control and will be specified in the DCDS Warning Order.

ARTICLE 105 - CANADIAN FORCES DOCTRINE

2. The CF will operate internationally as part of an alliance or coalition. Thus, CF **DOCTRINE** should be consistent, as far as practicable, with the **DOCTRINE** of major allies to provide the capacity to conduct combined operations.

3. Operational effectiveness of the CF depends on the development of **DOCTRINE** and sufficient personnel, training and equipment to employ it effectively. Procedures should be developed from **DOCTRINE** so that they will be suitable for use in any operation, with only minor changes to cater for different command structures or variations in force levels, structures and/or capabilities.

Annex C

Additional Comments and Recommendations on Supporting Operations

Figure C-1 on the following page shows a new organizational chart reflecting the suggested changes.

Due to the use of space sensors in support of strategic aerospace surveillance and reconnaissance, the term supporting air operations should be changed to "supporting aerospace operations".

Since some missions, such as parachute assaults, airborne operations and special operations[32] are actively involved in combat operations, to label them as "non-combat air operations"[33] is too restrictive.

The organizational chart for supporting air operations is inaccurate. It shows "supporting air reconnaissance" vice "supporting air [aerospace] operations".[34]

Combat Search and Rescue (CSAR) is not properly addressed.[35] CSAR is as valid a mission as Search and Rescue. If CSAR is to be addressed at lower level doctrine, then it needs to be mentioned at this level. Therefore, search and rescue operations should be enlarged to include CSAR as supporting aerospace operation.

While escort can be used during both offensive and defensive operations, *Out of the Sun* identifies it as being strictly a defensive counter-air role.[36] In addition to the traditional DCA role of escort, it is also used during OCA missions. When doing so, escort has a defensive role within an offensive umbrella. Conceivably, escorts could also be used during other missions/ operations such as during strategic offensive operations or in support of CSAR mission. Consequently, consideration should be given to include escort both under DCA and supporting aerospace operations.

Aerospace Doctrine 175

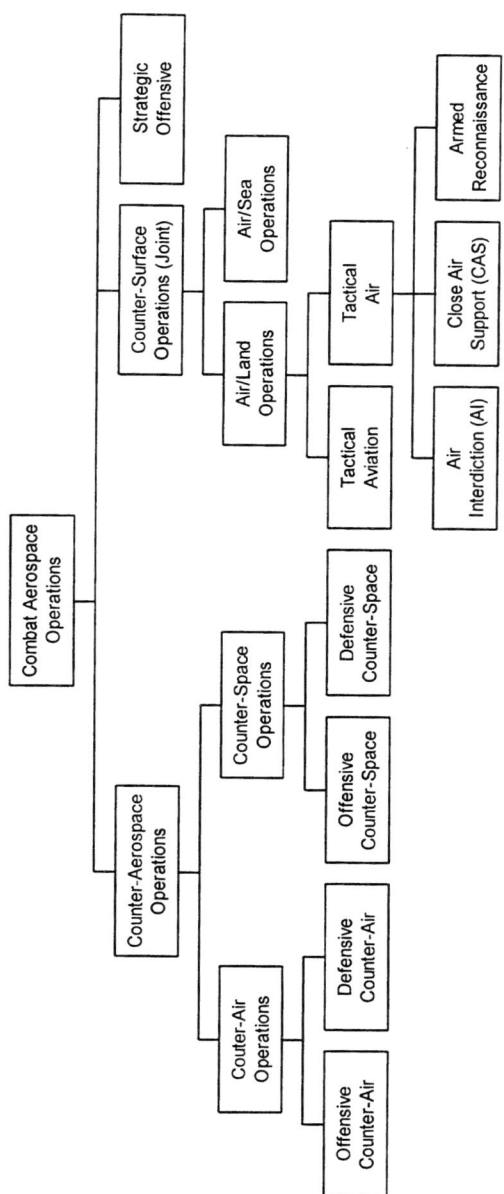

Figure C-1. Combat Aerospace Operations

Notes to Annexes

1. Canadian Forces, *Out of the Sun* (Winnipeg: Craig Kelman & Associates Ltd, undated), p 19.
2. Dr. James Mowbray, "Air Force Doctrine Problems: 1926 – Present", *AIRPOWER Journal*, Winter 1995.
3. Dr. Allan D. English, *The Evolution of Canada's Air Power or How We Can Learn from History* (presented to the Air Command Air Power Conference, Winnipeg, July 1997), p 2.
4. Squadron Leader S.A. MacKenzie, *Strategic Airpower Doctrine for Small Air Forces*, (Canberra, Australia: Air Power Study Centre, RAAF Base Fairbairn, 1994), p xii.
5. AAP-1000 *The Airpower Manual*, Second Edition, p 31.
6. Basic Aerospace Doctrine for the United States Airforce, p 8.
7. Group Captain N.E. Taylor, *The Importance of Air Power Within the 21th Century*, Air Clues, July 1992, p 1.
8. Allan English, *Air Power: The Evolution of Air Doctrine or Beware of Air Doctrine*, p 4.
9. Canadian Forces, *Out of the Sun*, p 1.
10. Mowbray, "Air Force Doctrine Problems".
11. Dr Larry E. Cable, *Conflict of Myths: The Development of American Counterinsurgency Doctrine in the Vietnam War*, (New York: New York University Press, 1986), p 113.
12. English, *The Evolution of Canada's Air Power*, p 2.
13. MacKenzie, *Strategic Airpower Doctrine for Small Air Forces*, p xiv.
14. Allan Stephens, Paper No 44, *Airpower Doctrine Revisited*, (Royal Australian Airforce, Air Power Study Centre, May 1996), p 1.
15. Royal Airforce, Air Power Doctrine, AP-3000 Second Edition, 1993, p 7.
16. Group Captain N.E. Taylor, *The Importance of Air Power Within the 21th Century*, Air Clues, July 1992, p 8.
17. Royal Australian Air Force, The Air Power Manual, p 27.
18. Major Robert J. Hamilton, *The Green and Blue in the Wild Blue: An Examination of the Evolution of Army and Air Force Air Power Thinking and Doctrine since the Vietnam War*, (School of Advance Airpower Studies: Air University, Maxwell Air Force Base, Alabama, June 1993), p viii.
19. Air Commodore E. Ludlow-Hewitt, 1934.
20. Raymond W. Leonard, *Learning from History: Linebacker II and USAF Doctrine*, The Journal of Military History, April 1994.
21. Col P.J. Taggart, DCOS IP&R, *A Working Paper on Proposals for the Development and Dissemination of Air Force Doctrine*, 3030-1 (DCOS IP&R) 19 Jan 1984, p 3.
22. MGen I.B. Holley, "A Modest Proposal: Making Doctrine More Memorable", *AIRPOWER Journal*, Winter 1995.
23. Ibid.
24. Canadian Forces, *Out of the Sun*, p 1.
25. Ibid, p 2.

26. MacKenzie, *Strategic Airpower Doctrine for Small Air Forces*, p 6.
27. Ibid, p 8.
28. Ibid, p 15.
29. Royal Airforce, Air Power Doctrine, AP-3000 Second Edition, 1993, p 7.
30. Col P.J. Taggart, DCOS IP&R, *A Working Paper on Proposals for the Development and Dissemination of Air Force Doctrine*, 3030-1 (DCOS IP&R) 19 Jan 1984, p 1.
31. Ibid, p 3-4.
32. It can be argued that aircraft involved in psychological operations are conducting non-lethal combat in support of the information campaign.
33. Canadian Forces, *Out of the Sun*, p 98.
34. *Ibid*, p 99.
35. Except for a non-doctrinal mention in page 61.
36. Canadian Forces, *Out of the Sun*, p. 70.

Inter-service Cooperation: Is It The Essence of Joint Doctrine?
Major D. MacGillivary, OTL. iG. T. Andrejews,
Major J. Blom, Major D. Fairley,
Major J. Gordon, Major D. Paquet,
Squadron-Leader. J. Samulski, and Major S. Sibbald

Introduction

NATO defines military doctrine as "the fundamental principles by which military forces guide their actions in support of objectives. It is authoritative but requires judgement in application."[1] It is of the utmost importance to military operations, and it must be carefully produced. Military doctrine is developed from three sources:[2]

    a. the lessons of the history of war;
    b. theory, which is the outcome of strategic thought, and;
    c. demonstrated or desired technological developments.

Lessons on the history of war include those learned from previous military operations. While this learning may not be enough to ensure success in any future operation, the knowledge gained may allow military leaders to avoid repetition of their predecessors' errors. Doctrine has been developed, followed, modified and adapted over many decades to meet the needs of the armed forces. This evolutionary process is a natural one; it is both desirable and necessary.

The doctrines of the army, navy and air force (and, where applicable, the marines) have been formulated and have evolved at drastically different paces. One of the primary causes for this variance may be linked to the age and experience of each component. As the youngest service, the air force has had the least amount of time to consolidate its truths.

The changing nature of service doctrines highlights the need for joint doctrine. The Canadian Forces defines 'joint' as "activities, operations, organizations, etc., in which elements of more than one service of the same nation participate."[3] CF operations normally involve elements of at least two environments, as no single component is best suited to achieve all objectives. The realization that each service has strengths and weaknesses is self-evident and occasions little debate. It logically follows that highly professional military personnel employing sound reasoning would then optimize military operations to best take advantage of the strengths and avoid the weaknesses of the various services.

This is not easily done, however. By their very nature, joint operations are not as simple as single-service operations. Joint operations must take into account more strengths and weaknesses, must consider more traditions and history, and, most critically, must deal with more than one commonly understood 'best' way of operating. To structure joint operations, a new form of doctrine is required. Joint doctrine is necessary to provide the fundamental principles to guide the balanced and efficient use of two or more services in the pursuit of a unified objective. To be truly effective, joint doctrine must be devoid of parochialism, be non-repetitive, use precise and clear terms, and address the requirements of all services.

Many problems arise when these prerequisites are not met. One of the most contentious aspects of Western joint doctrine is that it is parochial and service-centric. A common accusation[4] is that joint doctrine has been largely influenced by army doctrine. To follow this charge through to its conclusion, it has been implied that if army doctrine dominates joint doctrine then it must do so at the expense of the other components. The concept of army domination of joint doctrine creates what has been termed 'land-centric' joint doctrine.

The effect of joint doctrine being land-centric (or based on any other service doctrine for that matter) would be the less-than-optimal employment of forces during joint operations. An optimal joint arrangement is one that relies on the best possible service strengths and guards service weaknesses to maximize the probability of success and minimize costs. A sub-optimal force employment carries higher costs for the operation, in casualties or dollars, or even a higher risk of operational failure. This is especially important since:

   a. there is an ever increasing aversion to casualties;
   b. there is an ever-increasing pressure on defence budgets;
   c. new weaponry with longer reach blurs the boundaries between service spheres of influence, and;
   d. most future operations will be joint *and* combined (the latter referring to the participation of two or more nations).

For these reasons, Canada and its allies need sound joint doctrine. It is a serious allegation that our current doctrine carries any service flavour to the detriment of its jointness. Indeed, the mere possibility justifies considerable investigation. Such an investigation was carried out in the preparation of this paper. The authors concluded that current Western joint doctrine is not land-centric, but is held back by a wide variety of inter-service rivalries which prevent the creation of a truly effective joint doctrine.

An attempt to disprove the existence of land-centric statements in joint doctrine is difficult because it would be nearly impossible to examine every joint doctrine document and analyze every statement for joint balance. Thus a better method is required. In addressing the assertion that joint doctrine is flawed, this paper will:

a. analyze a series of articles which discuss the problems beleaguering air force and joint doctrine;
b. review and identify shortcomings in a sample of Western joint doctrines, namely those of Canada, the US, the UK, and NATO, and;
c. make recommendations that may benefit Canada in the further development of its own joint doctrine.

Analysis of Literature

To answer the question of whether or not joint doctrine is in fact land-centric, one must first examine the accusers' arguments. A survey of recently-published articles on the topic produced a list of four articles which summarize the essence of the argument.

The article that asserts most vehemently that joint doctrine is land-centric is "Closing the Doctrine Gap" by Rebecca Grant.[5] Grant presents five aspects of American joint doctrine that cause it to make less than optimal use of air power.

First, she points to the differences between the way land and air doctrine control airspace, missile defences and deep operations.[6] Differences certainly do exist between army and air force doctrine. This should not come as a surprise, nor is it a necessarily a bad thing. Service doctrines are currently undergoing a period of dramatic change due to pressures such as advancing technology and downsizing. In many cases, the separate service doctrines have not completely caught up.

Second, Grant objects to the army doctrine's claim that the army is "the nation's historically-proven decisive military force."[7] While this statement may be insulting to airmen and sailors, it is understandable when put in the context of centuries of army history and doctrine. Recent history such as the air strikes in Bosnia and Operation Desert Storm tell that successful operations are joint, not just army-centric. However, this divisive statement was taken from army doctrine, not joint doctrine. It is only right and natural that army doctrine be land-centric. The important issue here is that joint doctrine makes no such statement, and that it prevails over army doctrine in joint operations.

Third, Grant has singled out one joint publication, US Doctrine for Joint Operations[8], which states that "the Joint Force Air Component Commander (JFACC) has no geographical area of responsibility" while the Land and Maritime Component Commanders do.[9] To say that the JFACC has no geographical area only implies that he is a lesser commander in a land-centric world where holding ground ensures victory. Two-dimensional area has less importance in an air campaign than three-dimensional position, mobility or firepower. The joint publication quotation is a mere statement of fact, not a 'pecking order', and is both joint and efficient.

Fourth, Grant states that joint doctrine is largely based on dominant surface manoeuvre and that key air force concepts such as air superiority receive short shrift.[10] The importance of air superiority is an accepted fact on today's battlefield. The tendency for US forces to take air superiority for granted is probably a reflection of recent history, where the US has enjoyed complete air superiority in most campaigns. This statement is not a statement of air superiority's desirability or worth, but simply an omission of the obvious.

Finally, Grant asserts that "joint doctrine runs parallel to the army doctrine of manoeuvre, fires and force protection."[11] While these are originally land terms, one must examine them in terms of their utility to joint operations. For example, the operational art was originally an army concept. It has since proven to be very useful to both joint and pure air operations. The Army uses the term manoeuvre to mean "employment of forces ... to achieve a position of advantage in respect to the enemy in order to accomplish the mission."[12] This incorporates speed, mobility, firepower, and the ability to physically outflank an adversary. In the joint sense, manoeuvre (as opposed to attrition) is an approach to warfare whereby we are able to select a position to our advantage and force the enemy into a position to his disadvantage so that our strength can be brought to bear on his weakness.[13] This is an elegant statement of what the air force has always wanted to do, and actually clarifies the process by which air power is applied to the enemy.

Mark Gunzinger asserts in his paper, "Towards a Flexible Theatre Air Warfare Doctrine",[14] that the principal mission of air power is to destroy the enemy's air force, either in the air or on the ground. However, post-Gulf War analysts also concluded that the attrition of the enemy land forces was air power's most significant contribution to the joint campaign.[14] Gunzinger concludes that increased employment against land forces could open the door for ground commanders to have a greater role in planning and executing air operations. While this may be true, it may also be the most effective way to conduct joint operations, which is the ultimate goal of joint doctrine. It seems that it is not only the army that needs to avoid parochialism. The desired end-state can be attained most effectively by cooperative and coordinated employment of all services to the maximum extent practicable.

Although Gunzinger's article does not allege that joint doctrine is land-centric, it does bring out an interesting issue. It is apparent that there is a recurring theme of any one service continually expressing concerns over its actual or perceived importance on the battlefield. This animosity and self-promotion is generally the driving force behind arguments over which service is most important, or which is supporting and which is supported. In a joint world free of ego battles, this point would not merit discussion.

The issue of inter-service suspicion is further examined in James Mowbray's article, "Air Force Doctrine Problems - 1926 To Present."[16] Mowbray is highly critical of the air force doctrine development process. He describes a number of self-imposed problems preventing the US Air Force from developing comprehensive operational doctrine. He claims that the USAF has neglected air power theory from which doctrine should flow, and lacks an established and institutionalized process for the development and transmission of basic and operational-level doctrine.[17]

More important to joint doctrine, Mowbray asserts that the air force has a fear of committing itself doctrinally to more than it can in fact deliver. He states: "In an increasingly joint world, the air force must commit with clarity and without equivocation to what it can do for the theatre commander, the ground component commander and the naval component commander."[18] This agrees nicely with Gunzinger's remark that air power needs to focus more on its effects on the surface war. While air superiority is a logical and noble first objective, in the true spirit of jointness, sacrificing a few airmen's lives may save many more soldiers or sailors.

In contrast, Mowbray declares that the air force has a long-term paranoia created by its struggle for survival and independence. The air force "has become obsessed with winning the budget battles for hardware without the underpinnings of air power theory."[19] He continues: "This struggle for independence produced a paranoid state of mind in airmen that has been transmitted from one generation of airmen to the next. It is this paranoia that has been largely responsible for keeping modern airmen focused on 'survival of the service' rather than on air power theories, operational doctrine, and cooperation in a joint world with the other services".[20] Evidently the air force is partly to blame for the lack of effective joint doctrine.

Mowbray postulates that the air force is deeply distrustful of the army. By extension, the air force would also be suspicious of joint doctrine, and hunt eagerly for land-centric elements. Mowbray's paper reinforces the argument that army dominance is not the problem with joint doctrine. Instead, inter-service rivalries, poor understanding of the roles of the services, and the lack of focus on effects are the crux of the problem.

The previous three articles dealt with why joint and service doctrines are flawed. Major R. Hamilton's paper, "Green and Blue in the Wild Blue",[21] takes a different approach by examining the evolution of army and air power thinking on doctrine since the Vietnam War. His article presents some enlightening explanations for the way doctrine has developed in the United States.

Specifically, he presents a comprehensive historical review of air power doctrine in the US Army and Air Force from 1972 to 1992. He demonstrates that technological advances and the resulting changes to the way battles are fought have caused a convergence of army and air force thinking on the need for joint operations.

Hamilton states that it was not until 1990 that "a truly non-linear approach to warfare was examined and tentative acceptance given for centralized control of army air assets at corps and higher levels."[22] This agrees perfectly with the basic air force tenet of centralized control. Army thoughts about air power continued with the realization that "there is no universally effective mission for air power. All missions are important and their relative effectiveness is situationally dependent."[23] The more recent understanding that "air power is potentially decisive [on its own], independent of ground operations"[24] has led to "the general agreement between the army and the air force that air power can provide important, potentially decisive capabilities throughout a theater of operations when centrally controlled."[25]

This convergence of thought shows a significant breakthrough in the joint application of air power, though debates will continue over who controls air power and how it is best accomplished. Though the understanding is relatively new, Hamilton believes that increased jointness and decreased competitiveness between the services is gaining acceptance. If he is right, then joint doctrine has a healthy future, and its problems will slowly disappear.

The articles by Grant, Gunzinger, Mowbray, and Hamilton give a clear presentation of the bitter competitiveness between the services and of the infancy of air power. These problems have resulted in a lack of focused air doctrine and the reluctance of some army commanders to accept air capabilities as a unique and valuable commodity. Technology, financial constraints and the "increasing tempo, mobility and lethality of the modern battlefield"[26] have all increased the need for jointness in today's conflicts. By sharing their best concepts, service doctrines can strengthen each other and lead to a cohesive and effective joint doctrine.

Analysis of Joint Doctrine

Having examined some of the critics' arguments, the next place to test the thesis that Western joint doctrine is land-centric is in the doctrine itself. The joint doctrine publications of Canada, the United States, the United Kingdom and NATO comprise tens of thousands of pages of text. There are over 140 US joint documents alone. Thus an exhaustive treatment is impossible. Rather, an examination of key documents and those materials explicity addressing the use of air power will reveal any major non-joint concepts.

Canadian Joint Doctrine

Canadian joint doctrine is contained in "Canadian Forces Operations,"[27] which is developed centrally by the Deputy Chief of Defence Staff. It is authoritative in that doctrine produced by the individual elements must fall in line with it. Environmental concerns are fed into the joint doctrine through the Canadian Forces Doctrine Board.

On examination, the CF joint doctrine reveals a joint flavour. The first half (Chapters 1 to 17) of this publication deals with high-level concepts such as planning, command and control, and training, and carefully avoids any service flavour. The second half (Chapters 18 to 34) goes into more detail, and covers traditionally contentious topics such as targeting and aerospace control.

CF joint doctrine's treatment of targeting is simple and non-service-specific. In essence, the J2 (Intelligence) creates a Targeting Coordination Cell, whose role is to identify and locate threatening, high-value and high-payoff targets, consider each according to its value and vulnerability, prepare a prioritized target list with desired effects, and decide who will attack each target and when.[28] The process as described does not prefer any single service staff to perform the targeting nor any service's weaponry to service targets.

Canadian joint doctrine's approach to aerospace control is equally joint. The Aerospace Control Authority (ACA) is appointed by the Joint Force Commander (JFC). The ACA uses positive or procedural control to meet the air force's need for safe passage and the army's need for air defence and indirect fire airspace. The procedures are generic in flavour and contain little specific army or air force terminology or methods. The ACA is not pre-determined to be an air force, army, or navy officer but is appointed by the JFC according to the circumstances.

Canada's definition of aerospace power is consistent with that expressed by our major allies. However, the Canadian application of aerospace power is unique, as the Canadian Air Force command structure maintains command of all CF aircraft. Canada's consolidation of these assets under one command has allowed the CF to develop a single, consolidated aerospace doctrine which provides momentum in creating a true joint doctrine. Other countries, which have air assets scattered across several services are not so fortunate.

It is significant that both the Canadian joint doctrine manual, "CF Operations", and the Canadian aerospace doctrine manual, "Out of the Sun", were written within the same timeframe. The two doctrines were designed to operate together, though the joint doctrine is authoritative. Previously, Canada had been dependent on NATO for joint doctrine, but the development of a Canadian joint doctrine manual was to permit joint or combined operations independent of NATO.

US Joint Doctrine

The United States military recognized the need for jointness decades ago. As Dwight Eisenhower stated: "Separate ground, sea and air warfare is gone forever. If ever again we should be involved in war, we will fight it in all elements with all services, as one single concentrated effort."[29]

The US Forces are more doctrine-driven than the Canadian Forces, and since they are also among the largest and most advanced militaries in the world, one would expect them to have a large body of doctrine. When the Goldwater-Nichols Act of 1986 mandated joint operations and doctrine,[30] a daunting task was imposed on the US military: how to create such a large body of doctrine in a reasonable time. As was stated earlier, most doctrine has evolved over time rather than being created all at once.

Clearly, "since the Gulf War, there has been a deliberate US effort to write Joint Doctrine ... To achieve this result, the US Forces central/joint staff sub-contracted a good portion of the Joint Doctrine writing to lead agents ie. the Army, Navy, Air Force, Marine Corps and Special Operations Forces."[31] The problem this approach created is that each of the US joint doctrine publications has a distinct flavour, reflecting the viewpoint of its service of origin.

"US Doctrine for Joint Interdiction Operations"[32] is an example of a joint doctrine manual prepared by the USAF. There was a clear attempt to include an army perspective on interdiction – for example, inclusion of the term "deep operations."[33] However, comments like "the decision on where to place (*or even to use*) an FSCL [fire support coordination line] requires careful consideration [emphasis added]" displays an air-centric point of view.

On the other hand, the US Army wrote "US Doctrine for Joint Fire Support".[35] Instead of standardizing on joint terminology, this document uses mainly army terminology. Although it provides tables of common air force terms,[36] it does not even standardize within the same document. For example, the main text and glossary use 'SOF' for Special Operations Forces[37] while the air force table uses 'SF.'[38]

US air doctrine has been land-centric in the past, probably due to its roots in the US Army Air Corps. The same may hold true of other Western air doctrines. However, USAF doctrine now focuses on the effects of aerial operations, not the weapon system employed or the service that owns it, thus allowing for innovative approaches to air power employment without sacrificing combat effectiveness.

Interestingly enough, a review of air power doctrine in the US Army and Air Force demonstrates that technological advances and the resulting changes to the way battles are fought have caused a convergence of army and air force thinking on the need for joint operations. The US doctrine shows that both the army and the air force understand that the operational aspects of the fluid air-land battle across the spectrum of operations.

Because US maritime air and tactical aviation belong to the navy and army respectively, their focus has always been on the potential effects of air power on the surface battle. The same might be said of US Marine Corps air power.

A review of US joint doctrine revealed that it is far from being land-centric. To be sure, it contains flaws and hangovers from previous, service-centric days, but these are being detected and corrected with time.

British Joint Doctrine

British joint doctrine[39] is meticulously careful in avoiding service-centric concepts. Its general approach is to build upon single-service doctrines so that the air force conducts its business according to its own principles, even in joint operations. Although it makes use of army concepts such as manoeuvre, it uses them to improve joint operations, and in a way which does not contradict air doctrine.

British joint doctrine takes a broad definition of manoeuvre, although it makes excessive use of army examples, where the air element provides firepower in support of the manoeuvre action. It states: "Operational manoeuvre seeks to place the enemy at a disadvantage in such a way as to affect the campaign as a whole. Manoeuvre may be physical or conceptual in nature."[40] Despite this very broad definition, it goes on to describe the effect of firepower along with manoeuvre thus: "Manoeuvre may be accompanied by firepower to produce an operational level effect. This occurred in the Normandy breakout in 1944, where allied air power was used to assist allied ground forces to break through St. Lo, after which allied ground manoeuvre set up the Germans for destruction from the air in the Falaise Pocket."[41] "More recently, examples include the effective use of air power to strike targets around Sarajevo (Bosnia - August 1995) in conjunction with land manoeuvre so enabling progress on the political front."[42] Little is made in the main text of the Royal Air Force's ability to create the effects of manoeuvre by its ability to fix and divert the enemy, break his will and his cohesion – all attributes assigned to the 'manoeuvrist' approach.

Another potentially troublesome concept - that of reserves, or forces held back as a contingency - is handled in joint language, even if they are not traditionally employed by the air force:

> "The inherent flexibility of air forces to change posture quickly and effectively allows powerful reserve elements to be generated at short notice, without necessarily having to retain air assets uncommitted. Air reserves can be provided in one of three ways: firstly, an uncommitted force can be provided which can be introduced into the battle to increase combat power (this is rare although SACEUR held nuclear reserve air forces during the Cold War); secondly, committed forces can be switched from other tasks; thirdly, air operations can be intentionally constrained to less than full sortie capacity so that the ability to surge is maintained."[43]

British joint doctrine deals well with the nature of command at the operational level, defining ideal joint command and control relationships. For example, the JFC is directed to let his component commanders make best use their forces:

> "There must be mutual understanding between the operational level commander and his component commanders to ensure unity of effort. He should ensure that each component commander has the necessary access and that he displays no national or single-service preference. He must involve the component commanders fully in the campaign planning process and ensure each component is allocated the necessary resources and freedom of action to achieve their mission. As General Schwarzkopf remarked after the Gulf War of 1991, 'I built trust among my components because I trusted them ... If you want true jointness, a Commander-in-Chief should not dabble in the details of component business.'"[44]

Although the JFACC is usually co-located with the JFC, this is not to constrain air freedom of action, but to coordinate targeting and to control airspace.

It is interesting to note that those joint operations omitted from British joint doctrine are spread evenly among the services. For example, it deals effectively with joint special operations and joint amphibious operations, but misses airborne operations and naval fire support to army operations.

In summary, British joint doctrine is quite joint in flavor. Although it is not perfectly joint, any accusations of its being land-centric are unjustified. In fact, the cases where it favors one service over another do not single out the air force, but for instance leave out some land/sea operations (coastal bombardment) and some air/land operations (airborne). In other cases, where one service is handled differently from the others, it is with the goal of total joint effectiveness and not parochialism.

NATO Joint Doctrine

The NATO joint doctrine manual, "Allied Joint Doctrine"[45] (AJP-01), is very joint in nature. Indeed, at times it emphasizes jointness to the point of sacrificing refinement to ensure a joint flavor. At no time does AJP-01 state that surface manoeuvre is the dominant consideration, nor does it place army doctrine above air doctrine in any specific examples. When discussing campaign design, AJP-01 makes liberal use of army terminology such as lines of operations, decisive points, culmination, and tempo.[46] However, in the context presented, these are terms which best describe the activity, and should not be interpreted as a land-centric outlook. Indeed, there are references elsewhere to terms such as Air Tasking Order (ATO), Air Control Order (ACO) and the Allied Joint Targeting Coordination Board (AJTCB), all of which are associated with the air force tasking cycle.[47]

Another feature of AJP-01 which may dispel the land-centric charge is the existence of separate chapters on land and air operations.[48] The land chapter focuses on the coordination and interaction required by all services to achieve the overall objectives of an allied operation. The air chapter concentrates on the other services' awareness of airpower's inherent strengths and limitations.

In summary, AJP-01 is a very joint document. It reinforces the importance of all services to the joint objectives. It does not address any specific army concepts to the detriment of the air force's employment.

Overall, the proposition that Western joint doctrine is land-centric is not completely justified. Indeed, a detailed examination of the actual doctrine supports the opposite assertion; that in fact Western joint doctrine attempts to promote joint force synergy, even at the expense of each service's doctrinal freedom. The doctrines have a balanced, joint flavour. Furthermore, they leave the reader with the impression that there is a concerted effort on the part of the writers of joint doctrine to ensure that all services are represented equitably and that the overriding goal of supporting the Joint Force Commander outweighs individual service objectives. Where the doctrines fail to achieve this synergy, they do so in an even manner, at times defaulting to air force and navy as well as army concepts.

Misconceptions in Joint Doctrine

There is a widely held perception that Western joint doctrine is overly influenced by army doctrine, but the evidence does not justify this accusation. A study of current literature on the topic revealed no compelling evidence, nor did a study of joint doctrine. Where, then, did this misconception come from?

First, as was shown in Mowbray's paper, air force doctrine is immature and suffers from a long-standing fear of domination by the army. This may make airmen receptive to rumours that the army is attempting to govern their operations.

Second, given the context of a long history of single-service operations where terms such as 'lead service' or 'supported service' prevail, it is clear that this sort of suspicion would arise to protect service pride.

Third, with shrinking budgets and pressure to become joint, services will naturally build up defences for their interests and budget. This is done at the expense of both jointness and the other services. It appears that one way the air force has attempted to preserve its territory is to label any changes imposed by jointness as 'land-centric'.

Fourth, as Hamilton suggested in his article, the army has adopted long-range weapons (such as cruise missiles and improved aviation) that strike traditional air force targets, but on the army's terms and to meet army objectives. This has imposed a new way of thinking on air doctrine - an army way of thinking. The optimal answer is probably a blend of the army and air force doctrine, but from the traditional air force perspective, this is land-centric thinking.

Finally, the US approach to creating joint doctrine by parceling it out to the services feeds the inter-service rivalry and actually encourages accusations of non-joint thought.[49] This is probably equally true of other Western joint doctrine. Writers should be fully cognizant of the inherent capabilities of each component, but as joint training is a new challenge for Western armed forces, it follows that the requisite broad knowledge may not yet be in place.

Conclusion

This investigation, having shown that joint doctrine is not land-centric, also revealed another important fact. It is apparent that air force (and probably also army and navy) personnel have a profound misunderstanding of joint concepts. While air force doctrine describes the optimum way to prosecute an air campaign, it conflicts at times with the way the other services operate.

To achieve maximum effectiveness in a joint campaign, air force personnel must surrender some of their prejudices. A brilliant air superiority battle in the initial stages of a campaign may have devastating consequences to the land force. The point is not to choose one mission over the next based on service objectives, but rather to support the joint mission, embracing the concepts of flexibility, mutual support and cooperation. Ultimately, this will lead joint forces to victory. Some may oppose this subordination of air doctrine, calling it 'land-centric'. Ironically, in doing so they are employing 'air-centric' thought. The fact remains that no single service can operate independently of the others, nor inefficiently with them.

While the arguments presented in the papers reviewed lend an emotional appeal to the assertion that joint doctrine is land-centric, in fact they speak more directly to other, more fundamental flaws in joint doctrine and operations. In all likelihood, a comparable examination of the degree to which joint doctrine optimizes other joint relationships such as naval support to army operations would result in accusations of 'sea-centric' thinking.

There is no doubt that each service recognizes the value of air power and would like to control the employment of limited air resources to support its own campaign. There is also no doubt, however, that the unique capabilities of air power make it an asset best employed for strategic ends. After all, the very essence of joint doctrine is that it must optimally employ all services in the most efficient and coordinated fashion to achieve the overall aims of the joint campaign.

It is essential that nations have a sound joint doctrine that supports the coordinated and efficient employment of all environmental services under the control and direction of one joint commander. A simple way to reduce the complexities of joint operations coordination is to default to a single-service way-of-thinking. However, as pointed out above, this misses the synergy and efficiency available through joint thinking. Inter-service rivalries must be set aside and the best joint plan implemented to overcome the adversary. There is too much at stake to do otherwise.

At various times, individual services must be prepared and allowed to take the lead. To facilitate this, doctrine must be joint, balanced and practiced, and the other services must be prepared to follow that lead with trust. It really does not matter whether critics consider current doctrine to be land-centric, only that joint doctrine's underlying intent and implementation support the efficient, effective employment of military force.

What is important to gain from this analysis is an understanding of the necessity for joint doctrine to override single-service doctrine where the two conflict. Leaders and members of the various services of the various armed forces should always look at the bigger picture and determine how they can best contribute to the successful accomplishment of the joint mission. Their actions must be coordinated, conflict-free, well-planned and professionally executed. They cannot accept soldiers, sailors or airmen at the operational level—only joint warriors.

Canada needs sound joint doctrine. However, because some of our allies' joint doctrine contains serious flaws, Canada must be very careful when selecting which publications influence us in the course of creating our own joint doctrine. We cannot afford to be seduced into using joint doctrine that is already in existence based solely on an attempt to conserve the efforts of developing our own. We must also resist the temptation to follow militarily stronger nations, based on the conception that their size automatically equates to a top-notch product.

Rather than following others, what Canada needs is a focused effort on developing our own joint doctrine. Canada needs a Joint Doctrine Development Centre where the three service doctrines can be perfected and more importantly, where all service doctrines can be amalgamated, de-conflicted and closely coordinated. We need to consolidate our doctrine development efforts to share ideas, break down inter-service barriers and best use our limited resources.

In the end, when we develop our joint doctrine, we must avoid parochial interests and preconceptions, and always focus on effectiveness and efficiency. Joint doctrine must override single-service doctrine where conflicts occur and we must take all necessary steps to ensure that Canadian joint doctrine is sound.

Notes

1. Canadian Air Division, *Out of the Sun, Aerospace Doctrine for the Canadian Forces* (Winnipeg: Craig Kelman & Associates Ltd., undated), p. 1.
2. Australian Defence Force, *The Condensed Air Power Manual*, (Fairbairn: Air Power Studies Centre Web Site, 11 March 1998), p. 1.
3. DND, *Canadian Forces Operations (Ottawa: National Defence Headquarters*, 15 May 1997), p. GL-E-6.
4. Please see the following articles. Rebecca Grant, "Closing the Doctrine Gap", *Air Force* Magazine, Volume 80 (January 1997), pp. 48-52; Robert J. Hamilton, *Green and Blue in the Willd Blue: An Examination of the Evolution of Army and Air Force Air Power Thinking and Doctrine Since the Vietnam War,* (Washington:), Us Chiefs of Staff Joint Doctrine Web Site, June 1983. Available at http://www.dtic.mil/doctrine/jel/research_pubs/p186.pdf; Mark A Gunzinger, "Towards a Flexible Theatre Air Warfare Doctrine", *Air Power* History, Volume 43 (Winter 1996), pp. 51-57; James A. Mowbray, "Air Force Doctrine Problems 1926 - Present", *Airpower Journal* (Winter 1995), pp. 21-41.
5. Grant, "Closing the Doctrine Gap,", pp. 48-52.
6. Ibid., p.48.
7. Ibid., p.49. Cited from US Army Manual FM-100-5.
8. US DoD, *US Doctrine for Joint Operations* (JP 3-0) (Washington: US Chiefs of Staff Joint Doctrine Web Site, 1 February 1995).
9. Rebecca Grant, "Closing the Doctrine Gap," p.51. Cited from US Joint Publication 3-0.
10. Ibid., p.52.
11. Ibid., p.52.
12. DND, *Conduct of Land Operations - Operational Level Doctrine for the Canadian Army* (Ottawa: National Defence Headquarters, 1996), p. G-8.
13. Ibid., p. G-8.
14. Gunzinger, "Towards a Flexible Theatre Air Warfare Doctrine", pp. 51-57.
15. Ibid., p.55.
16. Mowbray, "Air Force Doctrine Problems 1926-Present", pp. 21-41.
17. Ibid., p. 22.
18. Ibid., p. 26.
19. Ibid., p. 22.
20. Ibid, p. 24.
21. Hamilton, *Green and Blue in the Wild Blue.*
22. Ibid., p.17.
23. Ibid., p.48.
24. Ibid., p.17.
25. Ibid, p.48.
26. Ibid., p.30.
27. DND, *Canadian Forces Operations* (Ottawa: National Defence Headquarters, 15 May 1997).
28. Ibid., p. 25-10.

Inter-Service Cooperation   195

29. Colonel J. J. Morneau, *US Joint Doctrine: Services Influence and "Disjointness"* (Toronto: Canadian Forces College Web Site, undated), p.1.
30. Ibid., p.1.
31. Ibid., p.1.
32. US DoD, *US Doctrine for Joint Interdiction Operations* (JP 3-03) (Washington: US Chiefs of Staff Joint Doctrine Web Site, 10 April 1997).
33. Ibid., p. II-2.
34. Ibid., p. II-15.
35. US DoD, *US Doctrine for Joint Fire Support* (JP 3-09) (Washington: US Chiefs of Staff Joint Doctrine Web Site, 12 May 1998).
36. Ibid., pp. II-14 and III-9, 10.
37. Ibid., p. II-14.
38. Ibid., p. GL-3.
39. UK MOD, *Doctrine for Joint and Combined Operations* (United Kingdom: Her Majesty's Stationery Office, undated).
40. Ibid., p. 2-6.
41. Ibid., pp. 2-6, 2-7.
42. Ibid., p. 2-7.
43. Ibid., p. 6-11
44. Ibid., p. 5-4, 5-5.
45. NATO, *Allied Joint Doctrine* (Brussels: NATO, 1 September 1998).
46. Ibid., Chapter 3 Section III paragraph 0308.
47. Ibid., Chapter 8 Section V paragraph 0820(d).
48. Ibid., Chapters 7 and 8.
49. Morneau, *US Joint Doctrine*, p. 2.